Royal Malaysian Air Force

BABAK TAGHVAEE

KEY
Books

AIR FORCES SERIES, VOLUME 11

Front cover image: M52-03 is one of 18 Su-30MKMs. It is equipped with a pair of powerful KNIRTI SAP-518 jamming pods installed on its wingtips, which can protect the aircraft from surface-to-air and air-to-air missiles. (Babak Taghvaee)

Title page image: M55-08 is one of 12 EC725AP CSAR helicopters from the RMAF, and is in use by No.10 Skuadron (squadron). (Babak Taghvaee)

Contents page image: M30-11 (c/n 5309), a C-130H-30 Hercules tactical airlift aircraft from the Royal Malaysian Air Force's (RMAF) No.20 Skuadron, flies over Kuala Lumpur during the Malaysian Army's 80th Anniversary Parade on 21 September 2013. (Babak Taghvaee)

Back cover image: M45-06 is one of the eight F/A-18D Block 50s. It is equipped with F404-GE-402 EPE Turbofan engines, which provide more thrust than those installed on older F/A-18C/Ds. The Malaysian Hornets are the most manoeuvrable and agile variant in the family of F/A-18 multirole fighter jets. (Babak Taghvaee)

Acknowledgements
I would like to thank Geoff Russell, Roberto Caprarella and Marco Valerio Bonelli from Leonardo, and Bruno Cabrini from Pilatus Aircraft, for assistance in the preparation of this book.

Published by Key Books
An imprint of Key Publishing Ltd
PO Box 100
Stamford
Lincs PE9 1XQ

www.keypublishing.com

The right of Babak Taghvaee to be identified as the author of this book has been asserted in accordance with the Copyright, Designs and Patents Act 1988 Sections 77 and 78.

Copyright © Babak Taghvaee, 2023

ISBN 978 1 80282 723 1

All rights reserved. Reproduction in whole or in part in any form whatsoever or by any means is strictly prohibited without the prior permission of the Publisher.

Typeset by SJmagic DESIGN SERVICES, India.

Contents

Introduction

Founded on 2 June 1958, the Royal Malaysian Air Force (RMAF) turned 65 years old recently. With 21 helicopters and 119 fixed-wing aircraft, including 26 in reserve as well as Early Warning Radars, Air Defence Systems, recently procured Unmanned Aerial Vehicles and other equipment, the RMAF spearheads the country's defence. It protects the country's airspace and helps its regional allies to deter threats in the region.

For more than six decades, the air force has supported the Malaysian Army, Navy and the Malaysia Maritime Enforcement Agency to protect the country's territorial lands and waters, and particularly the strategic Malacca Strait. During wartime and in peace, the RMAF's transport aircraft and helicopters have saved countless lives through participation in humanitarian and disaster relief operations.

In order to be able to obtain equipment, particularly multirole combat aircraft and their advanced weapons such as active radar homing air-to-air missiles, Malaysia has a policy to obtain and buy equipment from both the US and Russia. It has procured F/A-18D Hornet fighter jets and AIM-120C air-to-air missiles for them from the US, as well as Su-30MKM fighter jets and R-77 air-to-air missiles from Russia in the 1990s and 2000s.

Malaysia's economic crises in 1997, 2008 and 2009 have had an impact on the military's plans for modernisation of the air force. As a result, the air force lost a number of its capabilities, such as domestic fighter-pilot training after 2018. With the procurement of new aircraft such as ATR-72 Maritime Patrol Aircraft, TAI Anka attack drones, and FA-50 light combat aircraft and their pilot trainer variant in 2022 and 2023, the Malaysian Ministry of Defence is in the process of restoring some of that lost capability.

In this book, the history and current fate of 93 fixed-wing aircraft including 39 fighter jets and 21 helicopters owned and operated by the air force is explained in detail. In addition, the history of 26 aircraft currently held in reserve and other decommissioned aircraft and helicopters is explained, all accompanied by contemporary photographs.

Chapter 1

Fighter Force

Mikoyan-Gurevich MiG-29N Fulcrum A and MiG-29NUB Fulcrum B: 1995–2015

Today, the Royal Malaysian Air Force operates 18 Su-30MKM heavy multirole fighter jets, which are in service with No.12 Skuadron (Squadron) at RMAF Gong Kedak Air Base. They were procured as complementary fighter jets to its MiG-29N fighter-interceptors and MiG-29NUB combat trainers, which were in service with No.17 and 19 Skuadrons from 1995. Inferior to the Su-30MKM in many aspects, the MiG-29N proved to be a highly manoeuvrable fighter-interceptor, particularly when equipped with a combination of Russian and American avionic and weapon systems to meet the needs of the RMAF. In total, 16 MiG-29Ns (single-seat) and two MiG-29UBs (two-seat) were ordered by the Malaysian government under a US$600m deal (offsets US$220m including US$150m barter) in 1994 and were all delivered in 1995.

In the early 1990s, the MiG-29 fighter-interceptor became one of the most successful combat aircraft on the international market for fighter jets. In the late 1980s, many Warsaw Pact nations purchased MiG-29 Izdeliye 9-12. By the time the USSR fell, however, it was no longer capable of competing with Western combat aircraft. In response, the ANPK (Aviatsionnyy nauchnoproizvodstvennyy kompleks) MiG design bureau worked on two export modifications for the aircraft, which had significantly improved flight mission capabilities when compared to the older Izdeliye 9-12.

The new MiG-29 variants, developed for export in the early 1990s, were the MiG-29S (Izdeliye 9-13S) and the MiG-29SD (Izdeliye 9-12SD). The former had a large fuel tank at the top of the aircraft inside a raised dorsal to house an active L-203BE Gardeniya-1 electronic countermeasure system. In this respect, it was similar to the MiG-29 Izdeliye 9-13, which had been manufactured for the Soviet Air Force and Air Defence Force in the 1980s. Unlike the MiG-29S, the MiG-29SD had a small dorsal fuselage at the top, similar to Izdeliye 9-12A and 9-12B aircraft, which enabled the aircraft to carry 240litres less fuel compared to the MiG-29S in its Number 1 internal fuel tank.

ANPK MiG later developed the MiG-29SE, based on the MiG-29SD. It used the MiG-29S (Izdeliye 9-13S) fuselage and the MiG-29SD avionics and radar. The MiG-29SE had an active electronic countermeasure (ECM) system similar to that installed on the MiG-29S. The raised dorsal of MiG-29SE increased the weight of the aircraft slightly, which had an impact on its manoeuvrability. On 7 June 1994, Malaysia placed an order for 16 MiG-29SDs and two MiG-29UBs for use as pilot trainers.

The MiG-29SD had a maximum range of 2,900km with a full internal fuel load and three external fuel tanks, but with the addition of the inflight refuelling (IFR) probe, its range could be extended to a maximum 6,000km with just one inflight refuelling. Initially, the Malaysian MiG-29s were delivered without IFR probes, in 1995, but after completion of the design work and their production, 17 probes (including one spare) were delivered to Malaysia and were installed on the aircraft during an upgrade work, which took place in 1997 and 1998.

The MiG-29S's fuselage was small, making it impossible for the aircraft designers to embed the retractable IFR probe inside it. Instead they designed a special adapter to install it outside and on the port side fuselage of the aircraft's cockpit. The adapter added 65kg of weight, while the IFR probe added an extra 30kg. It could be installed in just one hour. However, additional modification works were carried out, including structural changes that would allow the transfer of the fuel from the IFR probe via the main refuelling pipe to reach No 1 internal fuel tank, and from there to other fuel tanks, including external fuel tanks during inflight refuelling.

The first prototypes of the IFR probe were tested in Russia between November 1995 and January 1996. Then, during a test flight on 16 November 1995, a MiG-29 equipped with the probe received fuel from CCCP-78782 (later RA-78782 and RF-94281), an Il-78 tanker aircraft from the Russian Air Force's 203rd 'Orelsky' Guards Independent Air Refuelling Aviation Regiment (203 GvOAPSZ), which is based at Ryazan-Dyagilevo. During the trials, the MiG-29 received fuel from Il-78 tankers at altitudes of 8,000m (26,246ft) above sea level, at speeds of 400–600km/h (216–364 knots). The first MiG-29SD to be equipped with the IFR probe was 357 Blue (c/n 2960536034), which belonged to the RSK MiG company. The tests proved that the IFR probe had no negative effect on the controllability of the aircraft and its performance.

As Malaysia had planned to equip its MiG-29SDs with the IFR probes, Lockheed Martin was contracted to convert four C-130H Hercules medium transport aircraft from its air force into KC-130H tanker aircraft at the AIROD facility in Sungai Besi Airport, Kuala Lumpur. For the tankers, eight Cobham 48 Series (formerly known as Sargent Fletcher 8) wing air-refuelling pods were purchased. Each KC-130H was equipped. The pod could be used to refuel the RMAF's MiG-29SDs as well as its F/A-18D Hornet multirole fighter jets and Hawk 208 light fighters.

The Cobham 48 series pod had an operating air speed of 105–250KIAS (Knots-Indicated AirSpeed) and could transfer the fuel at a rate of 150–330 US gallons per minute (568–1,249 litres per minute). It was equipped with an electrically driven fuel boost pump to compensate for losses in fuel pressure in the system. To be able to receive fuel from the high-speed baskets of these pods, the MiG-29S's IFR probes were equipped with the NATO standard MA-3 refuelling coupling; the same was installed on the F/A-18Ds.

Combat Capabilities of the Malaysian MiG-29s

Following their delivery, the MiG-29Ns had their flight instruments converted in the cockpit from metric standard to imperial units and all labels changed to English language (instead of Russian). They had a US-made AN/ARN-139 tactical navigation (TACAN) system, a GPS receiver, a VOR/ILS navigation system, a Raytheon IFF (Identification of Friend and Foe) system and a U/VHF radio transponder. As part of their modernisation, MiG-MAPO replaced the old N019 Zhuk fire-control radars of the aircraft with modern RPLK-29ME (N019ME) Topaz pulse-Doppler radar, which had improved capabilities for searching and tracking aerial targets, including an improved look-down shoot-down capability, enabling its pilot to simultaneously track ten aerial targets and launch two R-27R medium-range BVRRAAMs (Beyond Visual Range Air to Air Missiles) at two of them.

From the beginning, the MiG-29Ns had the OEPS-29 electro-optical sighting system, designed to search and track airborne targets following their infrared emissions with a field of view of ±30° in the horizontal plane and ±15° in the vertical in front of the aircraft. The system consisted of an IR sensor with a laser rangefinder capable of detecting and tracking small aerial targets within 200–6,500m (0.124–4.03 miles). The system can detect a fighter-sized target from a range of 15km (9.3 miles) and track it from within 12km (7.4 miles) range, feeding the data to the mission computer, and enabling launch of R-73E Infrared short-range air-to-air missiles (SRAAMs) at it, this being an optimum weapon for dogfights (close-range aerial engagement with enemy fighter jets).

To arm the MiG-29Ns, 250 R-73E SRAAMs and 131 R-27E/T BVRAAMs were purchased from Russia and Ukraine respectively in 1994, with deliveries taking place that year. Each MiG-29N could carry a maximum six R-73s under its wings or a combination of two R-27s and four R-73s using missile launchers. In addition to these missiles, each MiG-29 had a GSh-30-1 30mm autocannon with a magazine for 150 rounds. Autocannon was not available to aircraft carrying a PTB-1500 external fuel tank under the fuselage. In addition to the PTB-1500, the MiG-29Ns could carry a PTB-1150 under each wing.

In 1999, the RMAF showed an intention to procure the R-77 active-homing medium-range BVRAAM, which was extensively superior to the R-27R and could enable fire-and-forget capability for the MiG-29 pilots. The N019ME radars installed on the upgraded MiG-29Ns allowed the use of these BVRAAMs. With the completion of the missile's design and development in Russia, Malaysia finally ordered 35 of them under a US$35m deal in 2012, with deliveries starting in the same year. Despite the Malaysian MiG-29Ns being capable of using these missiles, none of them were delivered to No.17 and 19 Skuadrons and all were allocated for use on the Su-30MKMs.

20 Years of Service in the RMAF

MiG-29SDs and MiG-29UBs were locally named MiG-29N and MiG-29NUB due to being slightly different and improved in comparison to the original MiG-29SD and MiG-29UB respectively. The MiG-29UBs, which were manufactured between 1988 and 1990, received serial numbers (s/n) M43-01 and M43-02 in the RMAF, while the MiG-29Ns received s/n M43-03 to M43-18. They were all delivered in 1995 via the Antonov An-124 heavy transport aircraft, which transferred them to Kuala Lumpur. After assembly and test flights, they were flown to RMAF Kuantan Air Base, where they were used to equip No.17 'Typhoons' and No.19 'Cobra' Skuadrons. A year later, in June 1996, the MiG-29N had its first public airshow in Soekarno-Hatta International Airport, Jakarta, Indonesia.

In spring 1996, the MiG-29Ns participated, for the first time, in a national exercise in Malaysia named *Jagukh*. In April 1997, they participated in the joint exercise *Flying Fish 97*, which involved air and navy forces from Australia, Malaysia, New Zealand, Singapore and the United Kingdom. The 13-day long exercise incorporated 39 warships and 160 combat aircraft including 14 RMAF MiG-29Ns, and was one of the most ambitious exercises in the history of Malaysia's Armed Forces. The exercise ended at Tioman Island, off Malaysia, in the South China Sea. During the exercise, two KC-130Hs from the RMAF refuelled MiG-29Ns, allowing them to fly a long-distance mission and even simulate long combat air patrols. With its MiG-29Ns, F/A-18Ds and KC-130Hs (C-130Ts), Malaysia became a more influential regional player among the ASEAN countries.

In 1996, MiG-29Ns replaced the F-5Es in the air-defence role so the country had an air-defence capability 24 hours a day in all weather conditions. The MiG-29Ns and MiG-29NUBs were manufactured with US- and British-made avionic systems, Canadian-built flight simulators and an Indian-designed training system for its pilots and ground crews. In addition to the 18 aircraft, two additional MiG-29UBs were delivered to be used as ground trainers only.

As a part of the US$220m in offsets for the MiG-29 order, MIG-MAPO established Aerospace Technology Systems Corporation (ATSC), which was responsible for the maintenance and overhaul of the RMAF's Russian aircraft ground equipment and also acted as a regional maintenance centre for the Malaysian MiG-29s. After the MiG-29Ns and MiG-29NUBs had their Meantime Between Overhaul (MTBO) reached in 1998, they underwent depot maintenance at ATSC. Under a US$34.4m contract signed on 16 October 1997, MiG-MAPO carried out modernisation of the aircraft at the ATSC facility in Malaysia during depot maintenance. The first two upgraded MiG-29s were delivered to the RMAF in May 1998, at the official opening ceremony of the MiG-29 regional service centre. The remaining 16 MiG-29s were overhauled by the end of 1998 and were returned by mid-1999.

At the request of the RMAF, the MiG-29s had their airframes and equipment adapted for operations in wet and tropical climate conditions. They also had a variety of systems installed, such as Western-made satellite communication and navigation aids. The service life of the aircraft, which was 2,000 hours or

25 years, was extended to 4,000 hours, while the RD-33 Series 2 turbofan engines were upgraded to RD Series 3 standard, extending their MTBO from 700 hours to 1,000 hours and their service life from 1,000 to 2,000 hours.

In 2001, the RMAF indicated its need for a heavy multirole fighter jet capable of conducting air-to-ground missions as a complement to the MiG-29N/UB and F/A-18D fighter jets. The RMAF studied two aircraft; the Su-30MKI designed and built for the Indian Air Force, and the F/A-18F Super Hornet, a heavier multirole combat aircraft (MRCA) when compared to the F/A-18D. Subsequently, the Su-30MKI was selected over the Super Hornet and 18 were ordered on 5 August 2003, with deliveries starting in 2007. The Malaysian Sukhois were slightly different to the Indian Su-30MKIs in terms of avionics, weapons and self-protection systems so were called Su-30MKM (last 'M' suffix stands for Malaysia).

The RMAF continued operating MiG-29N/UBs for nine more years after the delivery of the Su-30MKMs. Alongside the Su-30MKMs and the F/A-18Ds, they participated in several national and international exercises each year, including *Cope Taufan*. During the *Cope Taufan-12* live-flying exercise held with the US Air Force, at least two MiG-29Ns, with s/n M43-04 and M43-11, participated. They were deployed to Butterworth Air Base, near Penang Island, from where they participated in various dissimilar air combat tactic (DACT) training missions against the locally based F/A-18Ds as well as the USAF's F-15C/Ds Eagle air-superiority fighter jets from the 67th Fighter Squadron, which were deployed from Kadena Air Base, Japan, in April 2012.

As the flying hours of the Malaysian MiG-29s began to reach their limit in 2009, studies began for the procurement of a replacement for them. In that year, it was announced that as each aircraft retired from service, it would save US$75m each year, as that was the annual cost of the fleet's maintenance. Subsequently, several aircraft were tested and evaluated, including the JAS-39C Gripen and Dassault Rafale B/C, but no order was placed and the aircraft were finally phased out, being in storage at the end of 2015.

Before MiG-29 operations ceased, the MiG-29Ns with s/n M43-03, M43-04 and M43-11 and a MiG-29NUB with s/n M43-02 participated in Exercise *Cope Taufan-14*, which was held at Butterworth Air Base between 6 and 20 June 2014. The exercise included 42 aircraft and two helicopters. Two S-61 Nuri helicopters as well as 18 fixed-wing aircraft, comprising four Su-30MKMs, four MiG-29s, two F/A-18Ds, two Hawk 108s, two Hawk 208s, three C-130H-30s and a CN-235M-220 were from the RMAF, while the USAF provided six F-22As from the Hawaii National Guard's 199th Fighter Squadron, eight F-15Cs from the Massachusetts National Guard's 131st Fighter Squadron, plus three C-17As, two C-130Hs and three MC-130Hs.

In early 2015, the number of airworthy MiG-29s dropped to just six, and by June 2015, just four MiG-29Ns were kept fully mission-capable and ready for quick reaction alert at the Kuantan Air Base, while a MiG-29NUB was used for training purposes to keep pilots up to date. On 1 June 2015, during the 57th Anniversary ceremony of the RMAF at Kuantan, the air force's commander-in-chief at that time, General Tan Sri Dato' Seri, announced that the MiG-29Ns would be upgraded to MiG-29SMT standard and would remain in service until at least 2020. However, they were all in storage by the end of 2015.

The RMAF has lost two of its MiG-29s, both single-seaters. M43-17 crashed on 3 September 1998 due to a hydraulic system failure attributed to the aircraft's battery. The crash was non-fatal. Subsequent inspections of all other MiG-29s indicated that the batteries didn't meet the manufacturer's specifications. M43-07 was lost on 9 November 2004, when it crashed into Ketengah Perwira palm oil plantation, around 30km northwest of Kuantan Air Base, due to an engine fire shortly after take-off. Its pilot, Major Fajim Mohamad Mustafa, ejected safely and survived.

A RMAF MiG-29N Fulcrum with s/n M43-11 taxis after landing during the first full day of flying in *Cope Taufan-2012* at Butterworth on 4 April 2012. *Cope Taufan*, the biennial live flying exercise between the USAF and RMAF, included dissimilar basic fighter manoeuvres and dissimilar air-combat tactics training. (USAF photo/ Master Sgt Matt Summers)

RMAF MiG-29N with s/n M43-04 departs Butterworth Air Base during Exercise *Cope Taufan-12* on 5 April 2012. (USAF photo/Master Sgt Matt Summers)

A RMAF MiG-29NUB Fulcrum with s/n M43-02 lands at RMAF Air Base Butterworth, Malaysia, on 11 June 2014, after flying an exercise sortie in support of *Cope Taufan-2014*. *Cope Taufan* was a biennial aerial combat exercise designed to increase the combat readiness and inter-operability of the USAF and Royal Malaysian Air Force. (USAF photo by Tech Sgt Jason Robertson)

A pair of F-15C Eagles from Massachusetts Air National Guard's 131st Fighter Squadron (USAF) and a pair of RMAF MiG-29Ns taxi to take off during *Cope Taufan-14* at Butterworth, Malaysia, on 11 June 2014. (US Air Force)

Crew and pilots from US Navy Strike Fighter Squadrons (VFA) 102, 192 and 195 pose with their counterparts from the RMAF No.6, 17 and 19 Squadrons in front of an RMAF MiG-29 (left), an RMAF Hawk Mk 208 (centre), and an F/A-18F Super Hornet, during an aircraft display and photo session that wrapped up a ten-day combined air exercise. (US Navy photo by Lt Chuck Bell)

During their career in the RMAF, the MiG-29s were used by an aerobatic display team formed of instructor pilots from No.17 and 19 Skuadrons. The team used four MiG-29s for display flights and had two more as spares. The team, known as 'Taufan Ganas', performed for the first time in 2001 inside Malaysia and had its first international debut during the Brunei International Defence Exhibition (BRIDEX). It performed during the Formula One 'Petronas' Malaysian Grand Prix at the Sepang International Circuit and also during LIMA airshows at Langkawi Islands. Its last display was performed during the LIMA-13 airshow between 26 and 30 March 2013.

Despite being stored for almost eight years, the MiG-29N/NUBs are serviced and kept in good condition in order to be sold or restored. At least two are in use for training technical students at Kuantan, while the rest are kept in a storage facility of ATSC under controlled temperature and humidity. As they are still kept in reserve, none were ever cleared for display at the RMAF Museum, which was located at the closed Sungai Besi airfield, Kuala Lumpur until recently.

Sukhoi Su-30MKM Flanker H: 2006–Today

In 2006 and 2007, the RMAF received 18 Su-30MKM multirole heavy fighter jets, which had been ordered in 2003. Designed and developed by the Russian Irkut Corporation, the Su-30MKM was based on India's Su-30MKI platform but with slightly different avionics and self-protection systems. The RMAF's Su-30MKMs are equipped with canards, thrust-vectoring and a long-range phased-array radar, enabling this two-seater aircraft to have an air-superiority role as well as ground-attack capabilities.

In 1994, Malaysia acquired 16 MiG-29N fighter interceptors and two MiG-29NUB combat trainers, with deliveries taking place in 1995 and 1996. In addition, eight F/A-18D Hornet two-seat multirole fighter jets were purchased, which relieved the RMAF's F-5E/F Tiger II fighter jets from air defence and a variety of other roles. The RMAF's MiG-29s, in service with No.17 and 19 Skuadrons, were upgraded and had their airframe and engine lives extended. Equipped with an inflight refuelling probe, similar to the F/A-18Ds, they boosted the air power of Malaysia significantly.

In 1998, Malaysia considered the acquisition of at least ten more MiG-29Ns from Russia and a similar number of F/A-18Ds from the US. However, its plans changed. Malaysia evaluated two other candidates before selecting just one of them to reinforce the RMAF's fighter force. Up for consideration were the Su-30MKI and F/A-18F Super Hornet. In March 2003, a Su-30MKI from the Indian Air Force participated in the LIMA 2003 Airshow in Langkawi Island. During the show, Malaysian Prime Minister Mahathir Mohamad was introduced to the aircraft, and several RMAF pilots had the opportunity to test fly it as co-pilots.

Following the show, the Su-30MKI was selected, and an order for 18 of them, their associated ground equipment, weapons and spare parts, as well as pilot and technician training was placed on 5 August 2003. The total value was US$900m, including 33 per cent offsets. The aircraft Malaysia ordered were slightly different to their Indian counterparts and so were named Su-30MKM (M suffix for Malaysia). Construction of the first six began in June 2006, followed by another six by year end. Construction of the final six began in 2007.

Like the Indian version, the Su-30MKMs were built by the Irkutsk Aircraft Production Association (IAPO). While the Indian Su-30MKIs had Israeli-made avionic systems, the Malaysian aircraft had French-made systems, which included Thales Identification of Friend and Foe (IFF), Thales CTH3022 wide angle Head-Up Display (HUD), Multifunction Displays (MFDs), Thales Damocles targeting pods and Thales NAVFLIR systems. Eight of these pods along with these avionic systems were procured from France under a contract with a total value of €150m, which was finalised in 2004.

The French avionic systems were delivered in 2005 and 2006 and were installed by the IAPO on the Su-30MKMs. The targeting pods were delivered between 2007 and 2009. In addition, the Su-30MKMs were equipped with South African-made LWS-310 laser and MAW-300 infrared warning systems, a Russian L150-30 Pastel radio-technical survey and warning station, and wingtip-mounted Russian SAP-518 electronic countermeasure (ECM) pods.

In December 2004, IAPO began converting two pre-production Su-30MKIs, known as Su-30I-4 and Su-30I-5, into two Su-30MKM prototypes. The first prototype, which was made in Moscow, flew for the first time as Su-30MKK-1 at Moscow-Zhukovsky airport on 23 May 2006, while the second prototype, Su-30MKK-2, flew at the IAPO's plant on 9 June 2006. They were tested by the 929th GLIC (State Flight Test Centre) of the Russian Air Force at Akhtubinsk. The knowledge gained from the test results was used in the development of the Su-30MKM and later helped the IAPO to design and develop the Su-30SM for the Russian Air Force and Russian Navy Aviation.

The first serial-produced Su-30MKM first flew on 19 May 2007. Five days later, this aircraft, together with the second serial, which had not been test flown, were handed over to the RMAF during a ceremony at IAPO. After completing all post-production test flights, the two Su-30MKMs were airlifted from Irkutsk to Gong Kedak Air Base, 315km (196 miles) northeast of Kuala Lumpur, using an Antonov An-124-100 heavy transport aircraft, on 19 June 2007.

No.11 Skuadron (Squadron) 'Scorpions' was chosen to operate the Su-30MKMs at Gong Kedak Air Base. No.11 Skuadron was a former F-5 operator. From 1983 until 1993, when it was disbanded, the squadron operated four Northrop F-5E Tiger IIs, three F-5F Tiger IIs and two RF-5E Tiger Eyes with a primary role of conversion training and a secondary role of tactical reconnaissance. After the squadron's disbanding, all of its F-5s were transferred to No.12 Skuadron. To host the Su-30MKMs, between 2004 and 2007 new facilities were built in Gong Kedak, including 15 hardened aircraft shelters and an aircraft maintenance hangar.

The Current Fate of the RMAF's Su-30MKM Fleet

On 10 August 2007, the first two Su-30MKMs were officially put into service. Four more were delivered by the end of 2007, six more in March 2008 and the last six were delivered in August 2009. The 18 Su-30MKMs were serialled from M52-01 to M52-18. Subsequently, No.11 Skuadron, once named 'Scorpions', was renamed as 'Golden Cobra' when it was reformed. On 31 August 2007, the RMAF displayed its Su-30MKMs during the Merdeka (Independence) Day parade at Kuala Lumpur on the 50th anniversary of Malaysia's independence. A few months later, in December, the Su-30MKMs also participated in the LIMA 2007 airshow on Langkawi Island.

The Malaysian Su-30MKMs are equipped with N-011M BARS ('Panther') hybrid phased array radar, which has given them the nickname of Mini-AWACS (Airborne Warning and Control System). The powerful radar has a search range of 400km (248 miles) and a tracking range of 200km (124 miles) and is capable of intercepting a MiG-29-sized fighter jet from a maximum distance of 120–140km (74–87 miles). In addition to its air-to-air capability, the N-011M radar has air-to-ground capability to perform ground mapping and detect land and maritime targets. The N-011M can track 15 aerial targets simultaneously in track-while-scan mode, with four of these engaged at once via R-77 active-radar homing medium-range BVRAAMs. The Su-30MKM is equipped with a secondary radar antenna in the back, which provides 60km (37 miles) detection range for aerial targets.

In addition to the radar, the Su-30MKM is equipped with an electro-optical sighting system named OLS-30. It has an infrared sensor with a laser rangefinder and is capable of detecting aerial targets within a maximum 50km (31 miles) (if approaching) and 90km (56 miles) (if distancing), and minimum 3km (1.8 miles). The system comes into use for air-to-air engagement via an R-73E SRAAM.

To arm the Su-30MKMs, Malaysia ordered a variety of air-to-air and air-to-ground weapons. For air-to-air combat, 150 R-27RE semi-active radar-homing medium-range BVRAAMs and 250 R-73E infrared homing SRAAMs were ordered in 2003, with their deliveries taking place between 2007 and 2009. In 2012, 35 R-77-AE active-radar homing BVRAAMs were procured under a US$35m deal, with their deliveries taking place by the end of 2013. For the air-to-ground missions, 50 KAB-500L and KASB-1500L laser-guided bombs, 75 Kh-31A1 anti-ship missiles, 75 Kh-31P1 anti-radiation missiles, 12 Kh-29T TV-guided air-to-surface missiles and 13 Kh-29L laser-guided air-to-surface missiles were ordered in 2003, with their deliveries taking place between 2007 and 2009.

In 2013, the IAPO and the Malaysian Defence Ministry signed an US$100m contract for the maintenance of the Su-30MKM fleet, which took place at the ATSC facility, the IAPO's local partner. In March 2019, ATSC started undertaking 'preventive and restoration work' on the fleet once they reached ten years of active service. The deal was worth RM2.2bn MYR, enabling the RMAF to operate the Su-30MKMs until 2035. Before the heavy maintenance began, the fleet suffered availability and mission-readiness issues. In early 2017, only four of the 18 Su-30MKMs were airworthy, which increased to nine by the end of that year. The RMAF now had 12 airworthy Su-30MKMs simultaneously.

On 1 June 2020, the RMAF announced that the unit operating Su-30MKMs at Gong Kedak AB would be renumbered and renamed No.12 Skuadron 'Lightning' for historic reasons. No.12 Skuadron had been the last unit of the RMAF to operate Northrop F-5Es, F-5Fs and RF-5Es at Butterworth AB until 2014. This change took place in August 2020. Later, No.11 Skuadron was reformed to operate three Turkish Aerospace Industries (TAI) Anka-S MALE UAVs (medium-altitude long-endurance unmanned aerial vehicles).

A formation flight of two Su-30MKMs, two F/A-18Ds, two Hawk Mk 108s and three Hawk Mk 208s during the opening ceremony of LIMA Airshow 2013. (Babak Taghvaee)

Su-30MKMs have always been the star of the LIMA airshows. One of them, with s/n M52-18, is taxiing after a display flight on 21 March 2017. (Babak Taghvaee)

Every year, fighter jets from the RMAF, particularly Su-30MKMs, participate in a passing exercise (PASSEX) jointly with US Navy fighter jets whenever a US Navy aircraft carrier is near Malaysia. Here, two Su-30MKMs flying with two F/A-18Es and one F/A-18F from the US Navy's Carrier Air Wing (CVW) 11 pass above USS *Theodore Roosevelt* (CVN-71) in the South China Sea on 7 April 2021. (US Navy photo by Mass Communication Specialist 3rd Class Dartañon D. De La Garza)

M52-11 and M52-16, two Su-30MKMs from the RMAF, during LIMA airshow 2015. (Babak Taghvaee)

A Su-30MKM equipped with a Thales Damocles targeting pod is banking over Kuala Lumpur during the Merdeka (Independence) Day parade on 31 August 2014. (Babak Taghvaee)

M52-11, one of the RMAF's Su-30MKMs, during the 2015 LIMA airshow at Langkawi Island. (Babak Taghvaee)

Three Su-30MKMs, with s/n M52-09, M52-11 and M52-16, were deployed to Langkawi Island to take part in the LIMA airshow in March 2015. (Babak Taghvaee)

Four Su-30MKMs, with s/n M52-09, M52-11, M52-12 and M52-17, flying in four-ship diamond formation flight over Kuala Lumpur during the Merdeka (Independence) Day parade on 31 August 2013. (Babak Taghvaee)

Northrop F-5E/F Tiger II and RF-5E Tiger Eye: 1974–2014

In its history, the RMAF has operated 23 versions of the F-5 light fighter jet. Included in that number are two F-5B Freedom Fighter training jets (one shot down and another sold to Thailand), 15 F-5E Tiger II fighter jets (three crashed), two RF-5E Tiger Eye tactical reconnaissance jets and four F-5F Tiger II combat-trainers (one crashed). They were operated by No.11 Skuadron 'Scorpions' at Gong Kedak AB between 1975 and 1993 and also No.12 Skuadron 'Lightning' at Butterworth AB between 1975 and 2014.

The first group of F-5s, comprising two F-5Bs and 14 F-5Es, was ordered under a US$39.24m deal in 1972, with their deliveries taking place between 1974 and 1976, while the two RF-5Es were bought under a US$8.2m deal in September 1980, with their delivery taking place in late 1983. Under a US$25m contract, one more F-5E and four F-5Fs were purchased in 1980, with their deliveries taking place in 1981.

With the delivery of MiG-29N/NUBs and F/A-18Ds between 1994 and 1997, the RMAF retired its remaining F-5s, which were all in service with No.12 Skuadron. At the beginning of 1998, only three F-5Es, two F-5Fs and two RF-5Es had been left airworthy, while three more F-5Es had been used as sources for spare parts. The F-5Es, armed with the AIM-9J Sidewinder SRAAM (120 were purchased in 1976) and the improved AIM-9L Sidewinder SRAAM (35 were purchased in 1981) carried out air defence missions as a replacement for the CAC-27/Sabre Mk-32 (Australian-built F-86Fs), which were in service from 1969 but lacked radar and the capability to use air-to-air missiles.

The F-5Es were equipped with the AN/APQ 153 radar system with a range of 18.5km (10 nautical miles) for detection of aerial targets, while the F-5Fs were equipped with the AN/APQ 157 radar with similar range but with two scopes for front and aft-seat pilots. These 'weak' radar systems could not provide beyond-visual-range (BVR) air combat capability for the F-5 pilots, so these aircraft were only used for air-to-air missions during the day and in good weather. For several years, the RMAF suffered from an inability to conduct air-defence missions during night until the delivery of the MiG-29Ns and then the F/A-18Ds.

All surviving F-5s were finally retired from service on 10 November 2000 and were put into storage as operational reserve aircraft. Three years later, the decision was made to bring the three F-5Es, two F-5Fs and two RF-5Es back to service at No.12 Skuadron for advanced fighter pilot training and tactical reconnaissance. Three of these aircraft flew again in August 2003, followed by another one in September 2004. By the end of that year, all seven aircraft were restored to flying condition.

In 2004, AIROD Sdn Bhd maintenance, repair and overhaul (MRO) signed partnership contracts with Caledonian Airborne Systems, Northrop Grumman and Recon Optical Inc to provide equipment to modernise the RMAF's F-5s. Subsequently, between 2004 and 2007, two F-5Fs and two RF-5Es received minor avionics upgrades, consisting of the installation of new ejection seats and GPS navigation systems. The most important upgrade for the fleet was modification work on the RF-5Es to permit installation of digital cameras in place of analogue versions.

For 24 years, the RF-5Es' analogue cameras were the only tactical reconnaissance assets of the RMAF. Depending on the type of the mission, they could carry three different pallets of cameras in their nose section. The first pallet contained a KA-95B medium-altitude panoramic camera, KA-56E low-altitude panoramic camera, and RS-710E IR Linescan. The second pallet had a combination of KA-56E camera and KA-93B6 panoramic camera; and the third pallet was for LOROP (long range oblique photo) missions and contained the KS-174A camera. In addition to these cameras, RF-5Es also carried KS-87D1 frame cameras in their nose.

IGTEC Sdn Bhd, in collaboration with Goodrich ISR System, transformed the RF-5Es' analogue cameras into digital cameras, allowing the Tiger Eyes to perform surveillance in infrared and high-resolution format. Tiger Eyes also received improvements to the VHF omnidirectional range (VOR) and ILS systems. IGTEC also installed the electronic horizontal situation indicator (EHSI) on the aircraft.

The two RF-5Es with s/n M29-19 and M29-20 and construction numbers (c/n) RA1001 and RA1002 remained in service with the RMAF until the end of 2014, when they were retired without being replaced by tactical reconnaissance aircraft. Together with the RF-5Es, the RMAF received an External Mobile Laboratory Transporter for processing camera films and printing images taken by the aircraft to be processed by imagery experts and interpreters.

In 2013, the RMAF had three F-5Es with s/n M29-05, M29-13 and M29-15, three F-5Fs with s/n M29-16, M29-17 and M29-18 (two upgraded), and the two RF-5Es serialled M29-19 and M29-17 in service with No.12 Skuadron. M23-05 and M23-18 participated in the LIMA airshow for the last time in March 2013. These two aircraft, along with the two RF-5Es, remained airworthy. The F-5F was used for conversion pilot training while the F-5E was used to keep the RF-5E pilots current.

One RF-5E was kept airworthy while the other was in reserve. The last three RF-5E pilots of the squadron flew with them twice a month for photography training missions in 2014. On 18 November 2014, the Malaysian MoD announced that all F-5s would be retired by the end of that year. Subsequently, the last operational F-5E, the last F-5F and two RF-5Es, along with three more F-5Es, which had been kept in operational/reserve status, were retired in December 2014.

Currently, four of the F-5Es are preserved. Serial number M29-04 is installed at the parade ground of Alor Setar Air Base; s/n M29-18 is preserved as gate guard of Kuantan Air Base; M29-10 is gate guard of Butterworth Air Base; and M29-12 has been preserved at the RMAF Museum since 2011. An F-5E with s/n M29-01 is currently in use as an instrumental airframe in the School of Aerospace Engineering at Malaysia's University of Science in Pulau Pinang. Currently, nine F-5Es, three F-5Fs and two RF-5Es are kept in temperature- and humidity-controlled storage hangars with the possibility of restoration and reactivation or sale, until the delivery of FA-50 light combat aircraft (LCA) and TF-50A fighter in-lead trainers (FLIT).

FM-1902 is one of 16 ex-RAAF CAC-27/Sabre Mk-32 fighter jets used by the RMAF before delivery of the F-5E Tiger IIs. This example is now in the inventory of the RMAF Museum. (Babak Taghvaee)

This F-5E Tiger II with s/n M29-12 was on display at the RMAF Museum until it closed. (Babak Taghvaee)

The RMAF deployed one of its RF-5Es to Langkawi in March 2013 to take part in the LIMA airshow for the last time. This aircraft, with s/n M29-19, was retired in 2014. (Geoff Russel)

M29-20 was one of two RF-5Es owned and operated by RMAF. It is taxiing before a test flight in the United States before delivery. (Northrop)

This undated Lockheed Martin photo shows delivery of an F-5F to the RMAF in 1982. (Lockheed Martin)

McDonnell Douglas F/A-18D Hornet: 1997–Today

A few months before Malaysia purchased 16 MiG-29SD (N) and MiG-29UB (NUB) from Russia, eight McDonnell Douglas F/A-18D Hornet two-seat multirole fighter jets were purchased from the US. The contract for their procurement and associated equipment was signed on 29 June 1993. On 9 December 1992, Malaysia had signed a letter of offer and acceptance for eight F/A-18D Hornets. The Hornet was more sophisticated and advanced than the MiG-29, making it more expensive. There was a plan for procurement of 12 more F/A-18Ds but this was cancelled. The Hornets relieved the F-5E/F Tiger IIs from a variety of roles, including air defence and close air support, leaving them for use as complementary and advanced fighter pilot trainers and also tactical reconnaissance.

The RMAF's F/A-18D Block 50 Hornets received s/n M45-01 to M45-08. They were each equipped with AN/APG-73 radars and two General Electric F404-GE-402 Turbofan engines. The first, M45-01, logged its first flight on 1 February 1997. It was officially delivered to the RMAF at McDonnell Douglas Saint Louis on 19 March 1997. Four of the eight Hornets were transferred to Butterworth AB in Malaysia on 29 May 1997, followed by four more on 31 August 1997. The first aircraft was among the second batch delivered as it was tested at Naval Air Warfare Centre (NAWC) China Lake in the US. All aircraft entered service with No.18 Skuadron 'Lipan' (Centipede) at Butterworth AB.

To arm the F/A-18Ds, a variety of weapons were ordered, including spare 20mm M61A1 six-barrel Gatling guns. For the air-to-air missions, 20 AIM-7M Sparrow semi-active radar homing medium-range BVRAAMs and 86 AIM-9S Sidewinder Infrared-Guided SRAAMs (export version of AIM-9M) were ordered in 1993, with their delivery taking place in 1997. Under a contract awarded in April 2007, 57 of these AIM-9S SRAAMs were upgraded by Raytheon in 2008 and 2009.

For the air-to-surface missions, 25 AGM-84A Block-1C Harpoon anti-ship missiles and unguided bombs and Bristol Aerospace CRV-7 unguided rockets were procured in 1993 and 1994, with their deliveries taking place in 1997 and 1998. To add precision strike capability to the fleet, 30 AGM-65 Maverick air-to-surface missiles in two models (TV-guided 'B' model and imaging infrared-guided 'G' model) including several captive training variants were ordered in 1993, with their deliveries taking place in 1997. In 2005, five more Harpoon Block-1s were purchased as a replacement for five others launched by RMAF's F/A-18Ds during various exercises.

To increase their air-to-air capabilities, Malaysia ordered 20 AIM-120C-5 AMRAAM active-radar homing medium-range BVRAAMs in 2005, with their deliveries taking place in 2007. Back in the 1990s, the US had not approved the sale of these missiles due to their fire-and-forget capability, but as Malaysia procured similar R-77 missiles from Russia for its Su-30MKMs, the US government's restriction on sale of AIM-120C AMRAAMs was removed in 2004. In 2015, ten AIM-120C-7s, an improved variant of the AMRAAM, were ordered, with deliveries taking place in 2016. In addition, Malaysia purchased 20 AIM-9X-2 Sidewinder Block 2 SRAAMs, a significantly improved and advanced variant of Sidewinder-family missiles. These missiles, with a total value of US$12m, were ordered in 2013, with their deliveries taking place in 2015.

While the MiG-29Ns enabled the RMAF to carry out air-defence missions at night and also in bad weather, the F/A-18Ds enabled the RMAF to carry out air-to-ground missions such as due to night vision goggles and NiteHawk targeting pods.

To increase precision strike capabilities, Malaysia purchased six ASQ-228 ATFLIR (Advanced Targeting Forward-Looking Infrared) pods for No.18 Skuadron in 2012, with deliveries taking place in 2016 and 2017. This multi-sensor, electro-optical targeting pod incorporates a thermographic camera, low-light television camera, target laser rangefinder/laser designator, and laser spot tracker, and is developed and manufactured by Raytheon.

ATFLIR pods replaced Lockheed Martin AAS-38 NiteHawk targeting pods delivered in 1998. NiteHawk had allowed use of Joint Direct Attack Munition (JDAM) bombs and laser-guided bombs (LGBs). In 2009, 50 GBU-31 JDAMs, and in 2010, 60 GBU-10 and GBU-12 Paveway II/III LGBs were ordered, with their deliveries taking place in 2011. In addition to these bombs, the ATFLIR could increase the range of AGM-65B/G Maverick missiles when its camera was used for target detection and lock on.

Before delivery of the ASQ-228 ATFLIR pods, Boeing at Saint Louis was awarded a US$17,262,617 firm fixed-price order against a previously issued basic ordering agreement (N00019-11-G-0001) for the design, development, and installation of engineering change proposal (ECP) 618 retrofit kits for eight Royal Malaysian Air Force F/A-18D aircraft under the Foreign Military Sales Programme on 28 November 2011. A number of RMAF mechanics were trained for installation of the new equipment. Seventy per cent of the work including training was done in Saint Louis, while the rest including retrofit of the F/A-18Ds was done in Butterworth AB by April 2015. The retrofitted and upgraded F/A-18Ds were called 25X capable. L3 Link Simulation and Training supplied the RMAF with an F/A-18D Tactical Operational Flight Trainer at Butterworth AB for supporting the upgraded Hornets.

On 5 March 2013, two of the first three upgraded F/A-18D multirole fighter jets, equipped with NiteHawk targeting pods, on deployment at Labuan Air Base, together with three of five BAe Hawk 208 light fighters at No.6 Skuadron, used rockets and bombs to target hideouts of Royal Security Forces of the Sultanate of Sulu and North Borneo during an Operation named *Daulat*.

Joint Terminal Attack Controller (JTAC) teams of RMAF's PAKSAU special forces detected opposition positions and reported them to F/A-18D pilots to pinpoint their strikes using GBU-12 LGBs. Hawk 208 aircraft used Mk 82 and 83 unguided bombs and CRV-7 unguided rockets during close air support (CAS) missions. During their presence at Labuan, F/A-18Ds flew combat air patrol over Northern Borneo. Later, four Su-30MKMs from No.11 Skuadron were forward deployed to Labuan and relieved the three F/A-18Ds.

In 2003, the Su-30MKM was selected to be procured as the future heavy multirole combat aircraft of the RMAF. Two years later, plans for procurement of the F/A-18F Super Hornet were put on hold. As a result, Malaysia's F/A-18D Legacy Hornets have been kept in service for two more decades and have also been upgraded in the past ten years.

In the past several years, Malaysia has expressed its intention to expand its small but highly capable F/A-18D fleet. In August 2019, it was announced that the country was negotiating with Kuwait for the possible procurement of F/A-18C/D Hornets from the Royal Kuwaiti Air Force, which planned to replace them with more modern F/A-18E/F Super Hornets from 2021. Kuwaiti Hornets could provide RMAF with an interim solution for a MRCA, which was needed as replacement for the stored MiG-29N/NUBs. On 15 November 2021, RMAF confirmed its interest in acquiring an undisclosed number of used F/A-18C single seat and F/A-18D two-seat, multirole fighter jets from Kuwait. As of April 2023, no contract had been signed for procurement of the aircraft.

F/A-18Ds are equipped with retractable IFR probes, allowing them an extended range with the help of aerial refuelling from KC-130Hs. With the delivery of A400Ms and the removal of Hercules aircraft from tanker duty, Hornet pilots were trained to refuel and fly long distance to reach Darwin, Australia, to take part in exercise *Pitch Black 2018*.

F/A-18D pilots fly at 100ft altitude and 450 knots (833km/h) before breaking over RMAF Butterworth for landing after their sorties. This image shows M45-06 in March 2015. (Babak Taghvaee)

An F/A-18D dispenses flares over Langkawi International Airport during LIMA-13 on 21 March 2013. (Babak Taghvaee)

F/A-18D with s/n M45-06 is banking during an airshow in March 2017. (Babak Taghvaee)

M45-02 lands at RMAF base Butterworth, Malaysia, 11 June 2014, during *Cope Taufan-2014*. (USAF photo by Tech Sgt Jason Robertson)

Formation flight of F/A-18D (M45-02), MiG-29NUB (M43-02), Su-30MKM (M52-02) and a Hawk Mk 108 (M40-01) flying in formation with a US Air National Guard F-15C-41-MC (MA/86-0157) and a USAF F-22A-20-LM (HH/03-4052) over Penang Island during exercise *Cope Taufan-14* on 18 June 2014. (USAF photo by Tech Sgt Jason Robertson)

Three F/A-18Ds with s/n M45-01, M45-05 and M45-08 flying in formation during the Malaysian Army's parade on the occasion of the 80th anniversary of its foundation at Kuala Lumpur on 21 September 2013. (Babak Taghvaee)

M45-07 during the LIMA 2013 airshow. (Babak Taghvaee)

M45-06 and M45-07, two F/A-18Ds parked next to five Su-30SM multirole fighter jets of the Russian Knights display team from the Russian Air and Space Force during the LIMA 2017 airshow. (Babak Taghvaee)

M45-06, an F/A-18D, during LIMA 2017 airshow on Langkawi Island in March 2017. (Babak Taghvaee)

BAe Hawk 108/208: 1994–Today

Today, the RMAF operates five BAe (British Aerospace) Hawk Mk 108 advanced jet trainers and 13 Hawk Mk 208 single-seat light multirole combat aircraft in service with No.6 and 15 Skuadrons in Labuan and Butterworth air bases respectively. The former operates them for combat missions, while the latter has the primary role of combat aircraft or fighter-pilot training as an Operational Conversion Unit (OCU). These aircraft are surviving examples of ten Hawk Mk 108s and 18 Hawk Mk 208s ordered in 1990 and delivered in 1994 and 1995 as replacements for ageing Douglas / Grumman A-4PTM Skyhawk light fighter jets and their TA-4PTM combat trainers in the service of No.6 and 9 Skuadrons at Kuantan Air Base since 1986.

The A-4PTM was the most advanced variant of the A-4 light combat aircraft ever built. The aircraft dates back to 1979, when Malaysia procured 25 A-4Cs and 63 A-4Ls previously used by the US Navy and USMC. The RMAF had wanted them to be refurbished and upgraded into 54 single-seat and 14 two-seat combat aircraft. The US government placed a temporary hold on their sale, resulting in an increase in the cost of their conversion due to inflation. As a result 40 were upgraded, leaving the rest as a source of spare parts.

Finally in 1982, Grumman Aerospace at St. Augustine, Florida, was contracted by Malaysia to upgrade the 40 aircraft to create six TA-4PTMs and 34 A-4TPMs for the RMAF. The aircraft were selected from the original 25 A-4Cs and 63 A-4Ls. They were completely rewired and their wings were strengthened to have two extra underwing hardpoints similar to the A-4E. They were also fitted with overhauled and zero-timed Wright J65-W-20 turbojet engines. They received advanced avionic and navigation systems such as the AN/ARN-118 TACAN, and a Swedish-built SAAB RGS-2A lead computing weapons sight. They were also equipped with the Lear Siegler altitude heading reference system and an AN/ARC-164 UHF transceiver.

To carry computer and avionics systems, the A-4TPMs were fitted with a dorsal avionics hump. They were also equipped with a drag chute assembly below their tailpipe, a new bulged canopy and a large windshield wiper. The upgraded aircraft all received the PTM suffix (Peculiar to Malaysia).

All A-4PTMs were wired to use AIM-9 Sidewinder SRAAMs for air-to-air missions and AGM-65 Maverick air-to-surface missiles. The 34 A-4PTMs had s/n M32-07 to M32-40 while the TA-4PTMs had s/n M32-01 to M32-06. These six aircraft were ex-A-4C/Ls and had a 28-inch plug inserted into their fuselage for a tandem seating arrangement similar to the Douglas-built TA-4s. The TA-4PTMs were equipped with four underwing pylons. The first TA-4PTM flew on 28 August 1984, while the first A-4PTM had its first flight on 12 April 1984. Deliveries of the Skyhawks to the RMAF started in 1985 and lasted until February 1986.

All A-4PTMs were equipped with IFR probes, which allowed them to have an extended range, thanks to Douglas D-704 external buddy tanks, which could be carried by A-4PTMs and TA-4PTMs. When the A-4PTMs and TA-4PTMs were retired from combat duty in 1994, six A-4PTMs and TA-4PTMs remained in service, being used as tanker aircraft at Kuantan Air Base until 1999, when the KC-130Hs completely took their place.

Skyhawks had a very high incident and accident rate in the RMAF. Eight A-4PTMs and two TA-4PTMs were lost due to technical failures between 1985 and 1992. The first such incident took place on 23 September 1985, when the pilot of an A-4PTM with s/n M32-10 encountered engine problems during a touch-and-go at Kuantan AB, skidded off the runway and exploded. Its pilot, Lieutenant Khairil Asdri Baharin, ejected and survived. Five other A-4PTMs were lost on 15 March, 23 June, 8 September, 3 October and 29 October 1988. Pilots of four aircraft ejected and survived while Lieutenant Wahi Anuar Mat Amin, the pilot of the A-4PTM that crashed on 23 June 1988, lost his life.

In 1989, the RMAF planned to retire its A-4PTMs early following the high number of losses. Subsequently, in 1990, Hawk Mk 108s and Mk 208s were selected for purchase as their replacements, with deliveries taking place in 1994 and 1995. Before the official retirement of Skyhawks in 1999, four more Skyhawks were lost. Two A-4PTMs were lost on 14 August 1990 and 9 July 1993, while two other TA-4PTMs, with s/n M32-03 and M32-05, were lost on 30 July and 21 August 1992 respectively. Both were lost due to engine failure during take-off and landing at Kuantan AB. Instructor and student pilots onboard both ejected and survived.

RMAF's Hawk 108/208 Operations

On 10 December 1990, a contract was finalised for the procurement of ten Hawk Mk 108s and 18 Hawk Mk 208s with a total value of US$740m (20 per cent offset including production of components in Malaysia). The Hawk 208s were equipped with AN/APG-66H radar, the smallest version of the AGM-66 family radars, which are a medium range (up to 150km/93 miles) pulse-Doppler planar array radar originally designed by the Westinghouse Electric Corporation (now Northrop Grumman) for use in the F-16 Fighting Falcon. The APG-66H has a smaller antenna, to fit in the nose of the Hawk 200 family aircraft, and because of that it has a reduced range and capabilities.

On 4 April 1994, the first of the 18 Hawk Mk 208 single-seat light attack aircraft ordered by Malaysia flew at Warton Airport, UK. The aircraft, with s/n M40-21 (c/n 424/MS001) was delivered to No.6 Skuadron at Kuantan AB on 25 July 1994, while the first Hawk 108, with s/n M40-01 (c/n 415/MT001), flew for the first time on 19 January 1994 and was put into operation with 3 Flight Training Centre (FTC) at Kuantan, together with another Hawk 108 on 15 April 1994. Others arrived by January 1996 and were delivered to No.6 and 9 Skuadrons at Kuantan AB. No.9 Skuadron 'Cakra' was moved to Labuan, while 3 FTC and No.6 Skuadron moved to Butterworth AB. 3 FTC was reformed as 15 OCU Skuadron 'Panther' at Butterworth.

Just a few months after delivery, the RMAF encountered serious maintenance issues with the Hawk 108/208s, resulting in only ten airworthy aircraft simultaneously in service from all three squadrons. These maintenance issues had been caused by the humid and tropical climate of Malaysia. Subsequently, Hawk 208s were absorbed by No.15 OCU Skuadron at Butterworth, resulting in disbandment of the unit. Later, No.9 Skuadron was renumbered as No.6 Skuadron at Labuan.

Out of 18 surviving Hawk 108/208s today, five Hawk 108s and six Hawk 208s are in service with No.15 OCU Skuadron at Butterworth, while seven Hawk 208s are left in service of 6 Skuadron at Labuan. Five of them are operational. These aircraft play an important role in supporting anti-terrorism operations and air-defence duties, despite being subsonic fighter jets. Equipped with a Rolls-Royce Turbomeca Adour Mk 951 turbofan engine producing 29 kN (6,500 lbf) maximum thrust, the Hawk 108 and 208 have a maximum 1,028km/h (638mph) and 1,037km/h (644mph) speed respectively.

During Operation *Daulat*, Hawk 208s from No.6 Skuadron launched unguided rockets and dropped Mk 82 and 83 bombs on occupied areas of Kampung Tanduo in Sabah Province, Northern Borneo, on 5 March 2013 and a few days after that. At that time the F/A-18Ds from No.18 Skuadron, which had been deployed to Labuan, conducted similar missions with precision-guided munitions. They also performed air policy missions over the South China Sea until Su-30MKMs from No.11 Skuadron relieved them in 2014. Deployment of the Su-30MKMs soon ended, leading to No.6 Skuadron undertaking these air defence using Hawk 208s, which had been armed with two AIM-9S Sidewinder SRAAMs (wingtip mounted).

On 31 May 2021, 16 People's Liberation Army Air Force (PLAAF) aircraft, including H-6 heavy bombers, violated Malaysian airspace to evaluate the readiness of the RMAF. They flew over Kota Kinabalu flight information region (FIR) and were detected by an early warning radar at the RMAF's air defence centre in Sarawak at 11:53 local time. Flying in a trail tactical formation, with a distance of about 60 nautical miles between them, they changed their course towards Malaysia while flying over Luconia Shoals. As a result, two Hawk 208s from 6 Skuadron were scrambled to intercept them. They encountered them at 13:30 local time while flying at an altitude between 23,000 and 27,000ft with a speed of 290 knots (537km/h) in the Singapore FIR.

The Hawk 108 is fitted with FLIR, Laser Range-Finder, RWR and CMDS and has a cockpit with multi-purpose display and HUD, providing modern fighter pilot-training capabilities to 15 OCU Skuadron. Similar to the Hawk 208, it is also capable of carrying an array of air-to-ground and air-to-air weapons, as well as the 30mm Aden Cannon. Hawk 108s and 208s from 15 OCU Skuadron have a secondary combat role. While they are primarily used for fighter-pilot training, they are also used for maritime patrol missions for anti-piracy in the Malacca Strait in support of 18 Skuadron F/A-18Ds.

Within the past several years, Hawk 108s and 208s from No.15 OCU Skuadron and 6 Skuadron have participated in a number of national and international exercises. They are *Bersama Lima*, *Bersama Shield*, *Paradise*, *Elang Malindo*, *Air Thamal Angsa* and *Cope Taufan*. In addition, No.15 OCU Skuadron sent instructor pilots to Labuan to join pilots of No.6 Skuadron during close air support missions in support of the Malaysian Army and police during Operation *Daulat* in March 2013.

Retirement of Hawk 108/208s

Between 1995 and 2022, RMAF's Hawk 108/208 fleet suffered 16 accidents and incidents, leading to the loss of five Hawk 108s and five Hawk 208s between 1996 and 2021. Some were lost due to pilot error, while some crashed due to technical failure such as engine failure (four cases) and hydraulic failure (one case).

The lost Hawk 108s include M40-03 from No.15 OCU Skuadron, which crashed on 18 June 1996; M40-06 from No.9 Skuadron, which crashed on 2 October 2000; M40-07 from No.6 Skuadron, which crashed into the South China Sea due to an unknown reason on 18 December 2003; M40-08 from No.15 OCU Skuadron, which crashed on 15 November 2021 at Butterworth due to an unknown reason, kiling Captain Mohamad Affendi Bustamy and a student pilot; and M40-10 from No.9 Skuadron, which crashed on 23 July 1996. Five pilots were killed and three Hawk 108s were lost.

The pilots of M40-02 also lost their lives after the aircraft crashed near Chukai in Terengganu, on 15 June 2017.

Hawk 208s lost in service include M40-21 from No.15 OCU Skuadron, which crashed on 23 Jun 2005 about 800 metres from the runway at Labuan Air Base during exercise *A Thamal* (a Thai-Malaysian exercise), killing 26-year-old Captain Mohd Yusari Kliwon. From No.6 Skuadron the following losses were noted: M40-28, which crashed on 31 May 2006, 10 miles off Bernas Beach during bad weather, killing 31-year-old Mohammad Rohaizan Abd Al-Rahman; M40-35, which crashed on 4 September 2002; M40-36, which crashed on 10 September 1998 during an air-to-ground weapon manoeuvre over the South China Sea, killing 29-year-old Captain Jaidef Biaspal; and M40-37, which crashed on 4 May 2007.

The last Hawk 108 crash, on 15 November 2021, speeded up plans to retire the Hawk fleet. At that time, only eight were left airworthy at Butterworth and Labuan. The RMAF evaluated various aircraft to replace them, including the South Korean FA-150, Indian HAL Tejas, Italian Alenia Aermacchi M-346 Master, Turkish Aerospace Industries (TAI) Hürjet, Chinese Hongdu L-15, Russian MiG-35 and the Pakistan Aeronautical Complex (PAC) JF-17 Thunder. On 24 February 2023, KAI announced a US$920m deal with the Malaysian Ministry of Defence for the purchase of 18 FA-50 Block 20 for the RMAF's light combat aircraft (LCA) and fighter in-lead trainer (FLIT) and also Aermacchi MB-339 jet trainers.

M32-30 is one of two A-4PTM fighter jets latterly displayed at the RMAF Museum. (Babak Taghvaee)

A USAF F-22A-20-LM (HH/03-4055) is taxiing behind two Hawk Mk 108s from No.15 OCU Skuadron at RMAF Butterworth during exercise *Cope Taufan-14* in June 2014. (USAF photo by Tech Sgt Jason Robertson)

A formation flight of an F/A-18D (M45-02), MiG-29NUB (M43-02), Su-30MKM (M52-02) and a Hawk Mk 108 (M40-01) flying in formation with a US Air National Guard F-15C-41-MC (MA/86-0157) and USAF F-22A-20-LM (HH/03-4052) over Penang Island during exercise *Cope Taufan-14* on 18 June 2014. (USAF photo by Tech Sgt Jason Robertson)

A USAF B-52H Stratofortress heavy bomber assigned to the 2nd Bomb Wing, Barksdale Air Force Base, Louisiana, flies alongside an RMAF F/A-18D Hornet and a Hawk 208 in the Indo-Pacific region, 24 September 2021. (USAF photo by Tech Sgt Matthew Lotz)

A USAFB-52H Stratofortress assigned to the 2nd Bomb Wing, Barksdale Air Force Base, Louisiana, flies alongside an RMAF Hawk Mk 108 and a Mk 208 in the Indo-Pacific region, 24 September 2021. (USAF photo by Tech Sgt Matthew Lotz)

A B-52H from the USAF's 96th Bomb Squadron with s/n 60-0059, flying in formation with a Hawk Mk 208 from the RMAF over the South China Sea on 24 September 2021. (USAF photo by Tech Sgt Matthew Lotz)

Hawk Mk 108 with s/n M40-02 and two Hawk Mk 208s with s/n M40-31 and M40-34 flying in a three-ship arrowhead formation during the Merdeka (Independence) Day parade at Kuala Lumpur on 31 August 2014. (Babak Taghvaee)

This Hawk Mk 208 with s/n M40-31 is a veteran of Operation *Daulat* in 2013, with kill marks for bombs and rockets used during the operation. (Babak Taghvaee)

Two Hawk Mk 108s with s/n M40-04 and M40-09 and three Hawk Mk 208s with s/n M40-23, M40-25 and M40-32 flying in formation during the opening ceremony of the LIMA 17 airshow on 21 March 2017. (Babak Taghvaee)

Chapter 2

Transport, Tanker and Maritime Patrol Aircraft

Lockheed C-130H/H-30 Hercules: 1976–Today

In the years between 1976 and 1995, the RMAF received 15 C-130H/H-30 Hercules medium-sized tactical transport aircraft, which entered service with three squadrons. The aircraft currently in service with No.14 Skuadron 'Peaceful' at Labuan and No.20 Skuadron 'Cloud' at Subang (Kuala Lumpur) have been in use for three main missions, including tactical transport, inflight refuelling and maritime patrol. They have proved to be the workhorse of the 10th Parachute Brigade, a rapid deployment force of the Malaysian Army. They have supported operations of the Malaysian Armed Forces, airlifting personnel and equipment, and have played an important role in humanitarian disaster-relief operations.

C-130Hs were purchased for use as a complementary aircraft for the De Havilland Canada DHC-4 Caribou short take-off and landing (STOL) capable light transport aircraft of the RMAF. In total, 18 were received from Canada between 1966 and 1972, and 16 of them were still in service when the RMAF began operating C-130s. The first six C-130Hs, with s/n FM2401 to FM2406 (FM prefix stood for Federation of Malaysia), were ordered under a US$48m deal in 1974. They were delivered to RMAF between March and October 1976 and entered service with No.14 Skuadron (and No.20 Skuadron at Subang Air Base. Their serial numbers were later changed to M30-01 to M30-06.

On 25 August 1990, the RMAF lost one of its C-130Hs with s/n M30-03 (c/n 4674) in an accident. The aircraft skidded off the runway of Sibu airport during landing, due to failure of its Number 3 and 4 engines on its final approach, and came to rest among trees. A passenger died when unsecured baggage in the aircraft fell on him. The aircraft had 32 passengers on board, including a royal entourage, together with eight crew. M30-03 was declared damaged beyond repair and was scrapped on site.

In 1979, Malaysia ordered three more C-130Hs, to be slightly modified for maritime patrol duties under a US$28m deal. The aircraft, which were manufactured under the C-130H-MP name, were serialled FM2451 to FM2453 and were handed over to No.4 Skuadron in Subang in April and December 1980. No.4 Skuadron, whose primary role was maritime patrol and whose secondary role was tactical transport, was moved to Labuan Air Base. The serial numbers of these C-130H-30s were later changed to M30-07 to M30-09.

This stretched version of the C-130H was equipped with four Allison T56-A-15 turboprop engines. Named the C-130H-30, this extended aircraft was 15ft (4.57m) longer than the C-130H, enabling transportation of more troops or larger cargo inside the cabin. The increase in aircraft length was possible by insertion of an 8ft (2.54m)-long plug aft of the cockpit and a 6½ft (2.03m) plug at the rear of the fuselage. Malaysia ordered one C-130H-30 in 1990, with its delivery taking place in November 1993. The aircraft received s/n M30-10. Five more C-130H-30s were ordered in 1995, with their deliveries taking place between 1995 and 2002. These aircraft received s/n M-30-11 to M-30-16.

In 1995, a contract was finalised to convert two C-130Hs to KC-130H tanker aircraft at the AIROD facility in Subang airport. Under the US$23m deal, two C-130Hs with s/n M30-01 and M30-02 were modified for their new tanker role. They were each equipped with a pair of Cobham 48 Series (formerly known as Sargent Fletcher 8) refuelling pods. Both were redelivered to No.20 Skuadron at Subang after conversion. In 2002, another contract, with a total value of RM102m MYR, was finalized, to convert two C-130H-MPs from No.4 Skuadron into KC-130Hs at the AIROD facility. Once complete, they were delivered to No.20 Skuadron.

In addition to conducting military missions in support of the Malaysian Armed Forces, the C-130Hs were widely used to serve the public. In April 2009, a C-130H-30 from No.14 Skuadron, based at Labuan, participated in a 22-hour-long mission to transport Malaysia's second RazakSat mini satellite to Guam in the Pacific Ocean so that it could be launched. The aircraft was crewed by 18 people; the five pilots were named Captain Zeti Haryani Ismail, Major Hezri Hassan, Lieutenant Colonel Raja Mohar Raja Bahari, Captain Nazlan Shah Zainal and Captain Khairill Anuar.

Following the 2011 Egyptian revolution, the Malaysian Security Council issued an order to evacuate hundreds of Malaysian students trapped in Egypt in January and February 2011. Two C-130H-30s from No.14 Skuadron and one C-130H-30 from No.20 Skuadron were deployed to Jeddah, Saudi Arabia, where they logged 18 sorties to Cairo and Alexandria to evacuate Malaysian students between 4 and 7 February 2011. Each logged three sorties per day and each sortie evacuated almost 200 passengers.

On 18 June 2022, No.20 Skuadron was tasked to carry out a cloud-seeding operation (OPA) in the Bukit Merah Dam catchment area, Semanggol, Kerian District, Perak. This OPA involved the Ministry of Agriculture and Food Industries (also known as MAFI), the Malaysian Meteorological Department (MET Malaysia), the National Disaster Management Agency (NADMA) and the RMAF. The operation would benefit more than 10,000 rice farmers farming 19,058 hectares of paddy fields in the Kerian Integrated Agricultural Development Area (IADA) and 1,267 hectares in the Penang IADA area. To carry out the mission, four barrels of salt mixture with a load of 1,200l per barrel were loaded into the aircraft, which was piloted by the commanding officer of No.20 Skuadron, Lieutenant Colonel Faizul Hussein bin Dato' Ismail, and co-piloted by Major Zul Helmie bin Zainuddin and Assistant Pilot, Captain Muhammad Zulhilmi bin Nordin.

Evacuation of Malaysian Nationals in Distress

In May 2015, two C-130H-30s from No.20 Skuadron, together with 90 RMAF service personnel, were deployed to Prince Sultan Air Base (PSAB) in Saudi Arabia. They joined 11 other air forces participating in Operation *Decisive Storm*, led by Saudi Arabia against Houthi rebels (Ansarullah forces), which were backed by Iran's Islamic regime and which, following an armed riot and unrest, took power in Sana'a in March.

While some of the air forces involved in the operation were tasked to carry out strike missions against the Houthi, the RMAF used its two C-130H-30s to evacuate approximately 500 Malaysian university students trapped in Sana'a and Hodeida, Yemen. Following the evacuation of these Malaysian nationals, the RMAF used its C-130s to support the operations of the Royal Saudi Armed Forces.

From 6 May 2015 to 4 September 2018, a total of seven C-130Hs and 1,068 RMAF personnel were deployed to PSAB. Throughout the three-year deployment, one of the longest in the history of the RMAF, the force maintained a serviceability rate of between 50–60 per cent, conducted more than 500 operational sorties and training flights and integrated and acquitted itself. Concept, training and best practices adopted by the RMAF were put through the wringer and validated. Team leaders were taught how to manage the priceless human capital. It also enhanced interoperability between the Royal Saudi Air Force and other regional, American and European air forces.

The RMAF's involvement in Operation *Decisive Storm* was part of Malaysia's payback to Saudi Arabia for its financial support during an economic crisis. The RMAF's participation in the operation allowed No.14 and 20 Skuadrons to evolve as a modern, capable and formidable fighting force able to respond quickly to rapidly changing scenarios. The experience gleaned allowed them to grow and become ready to face challenges.

COVID-19 Relief Operations Using C-130s

The RMAF's C-130s were widely used for supporting people in COVID-19-affected regions of Malaysia between 2019 and 2022. On 18 June 2021, a C-130H-30 from No.20 Skuadron with s/n M30-15 airlifted food-aid kits such as rice, sugar, wheat flour and cooking oil from Subang to Labuan, to be given to people in villages affected.

On 15 September of the same year, the same C-130H-30 airlifted medical aid to Indonesia to help relieve those suffering from the COVID-19 pandemic.

On 28 September 2021, a RMAF C-130H-30 and an A400M flew from Subang Air Base to Kuching and Kota Kinabal, at 08:00am local time, carrying medical equipment and supplies from the Public Health Special Task Force known as the Greater Klang Valley Special Task Force (GKVSTF), following the COVID-19 outbreak in the Greater Klang Valley. A similar mission was carried out by another C-130H-30 and an A400M on 2 October 2021.

The Future of the Hercules Fleet

In November 1997, the RMAF had two KC-130H tankers (also known as C-130T), three C-130H-MPs and nine C-130H-30s in service with No.4, 14 and 20 Skuadrons. In that month, No.4 Skuadron at Labuan was disbanded, and No.14 Skuadron, now equipped with six C-130H-30s, took its place in Labuan. Out of three C-130H-MPs from No.4 Skuadron, two, with s/n M30-07 and M30-08 were selected to undergo conversion to KC-130Hs at AIROD under a 102m MYR contract, which was finalised in 2000. The last C-130H-MP with s/n M30-09 was absorbed by No.20 Skuadron and was mostly used for transport purposes. Four Beechcraft B200T King Airs with s/n M41-01 to M41-04 had already taken over the maritime patrol duties of C-130H-MPs at No.16 Skuadron 'Canary', based in Subang.

In 2005, Malaysia placed an order for four Airbus A400M Atlas heavy transport aircraft with a total value of €500m, with €400m offsets. As part of the contract, Airbus Defence supplied the RMAF with inflight refuelling pods, allowing the RMAF to use them as tankers. The A400Ms were delivered between 2015 and 2017 but, before delivery, the inflight refuelling pods of two of the KC-130Hs were removed. With the delivery of A400Ms, the remaining two KC-130Hs were completely stripped of their tanker duties and were used only for transport missions.

To keep the C-130H/H-30 fleet in service until at least 2045, the engineering units of No.14 and 20 Skuadrons have performed various structural inspections and necessary repairs during organisation-level maintenance, while AIROD has performed various upgrade works on the aircraft during depot maintenance or overhaul at its facility in Subang.

On 7 February 2023, the RMAF's No.14 Skuadron held a ceremony for successfully re-establishing Second Line Servicing capability. During the ceremony, 14 Skuadron unveiled s/n M30-08, a C-130H that had undergone a complete structural inspection known as ST-33 Years at Labuan Air Base's maintenance hangar. A few days later, the engineering branch of 20 Skuadron completed Structural Inspection 21 Years (ST-21 Years) maintenance of a C-130H-30 with s/n M30-16 at Subang.

The last known incident leading to withdrawal of a Hercules from RMAF service affected s/n M30-14, a C-130H-30 from 14 Skuadron, after it had a gear-up landing on 18 November 2017. As of April 2023, the RMAF had four KC-130Hs, a C-130H-MP and nine C-130H-30s in service with 14 and 20 Skuadron. Among these, just seven aircraft with s/n M30-02, M-30-07, M30-08, M30-11, M30-12, M30-15 and M30-16 were in operational cycle, while M30-04, M30-05, M30-06, M30-09 and M30-10 were under maintenance or awaiting service, and M30-01 was in storage.

M30-04, a C-130H-30 from No.14 Skuadron, is at Langkawi International Airport on 24 March 2017. (Babak Taghvaee)

M30-06, a C-130H-30 from No.14 Skuadron, is at Langkawi International Airport on 24 March 2017. (Babak Taghvaee)

M30-11 is a C-130H-30 from No.20 Skuadron and features at a Malaysian Army parade at Kuala Lumpur on 21 September 2013. (Babak Taghvaee)

M30-05 is a C-130H-30 from No.14 Skuadron and is at Langkawi International Airport on 17 March 2015. (Babak Taghvaee)

M30-09 is the sole C-130H-MP from No.20 Skuadron and is at Langkawi International Airport on 17 March 2015. (Babak Taghvaee)

M30-15, a C-130H-30 from No.20 Skuadron, is landing at Subang airport on 23 August 2014. (Babak Taghvaee)

Left: M30-15 is a C-130H-30 from No.20 Skuadron and received a special sticker on the occasion of the 56th anniversary of Malaysia's independence prior to its participation in the Merdeka (Independence) Day parade on 31 August 2014. (Babak Taghvaee)

Below: The formation flight of two C-130H-30s and a CN-235-220M during the Merdeka Day parade over Kuala Lumpur on 31 August 2014. (Babak Taghvaee)

A formation flight of a C-130H-30 (s/n M30-16) and a C-130H-MP (s/n M30-09) during the Merdeka Day parade over Kuala Lumpur on 31 August 2014. (Babak Taghvaee)

M30-16, a C-130H-30 from No.20 Skuadron, landing at Subang airport on 20 September 2013. (Babak Taghvaee)

M30-12, a C-130H-30 from No.20 Skuadron landing at Langkawi on 22 March 2017. (Babak Taghvaee)

M30-10, a C-130H-30 from No.14 Skuadron landing at Langkawi on 17 March 2017. It has jungle camouflage. (Babak Taghvaee)

Airbus A400M Atlas: 2015–Today

In the years between 2015 and 2017, the RMAF received four Airbus A400M Atlas tactical transport aircraft, which were ordered under a €900m contract (including €400m offsets) signed on 8 December 2005. The aircraft entered service with 22 Skuadron (reorganised as 8 Skuadron as of 8 April 2022) at Subang AB. These A400Ms have so far been used in various tactical and strategic missions, such as troop and cargo transport, air-to-air refuelling, medical evacuation (MEDEVAC) and humanitarian assistance disaster relief (HADR). During the COVID-19 pandemic in Malaysia, the aircraft were used for air delivery of medical aid to areas affected when commercial airlines stopped flying.

The RMAF received the 908E Wing Pod (for inflight refuelling) and 808E Hose Drum Unit (HDU) for the pods, enabling the A400Ms to be used as tanker aircraft and relieving the four KC-130Hs from 20 Skuadron of this duty. With these pods, an A400M with s/n M54-04 refuelled five F/A-18D Block 50s from 18 Skuadron (s/n M45-01, M45-02, M45-06, M45-07 and M45-08) on their way from Butterworth AB to the Royal Australian Air Force (RAAF) Air Base at Darwin, Australia, for participation in the multinational exercise *Pitch Black 18*, hosted by the RAAF and held between 27 July and 17 August 2018.

The first A400M for the RMAF was assembled at San Pablo, Seville, at the Spanish factory belonging to Airbus Defence in September 2014. Its first flight was logged there on 30 January 2015. It was the 16th A400M to be built by Airbus. At that time, ten A400Ms were in operational use across the world; six in the French Air Force, one in the German Air Force, two in the Turkish Air Force and one in the Royal Air Force.

After nine months of delay, mainly due to technical work and the redesign of some components of the gearbox of the Europrop TP400-D6 turboprop engines, Airbus delivered the fourth and final Airbus A400M to the RMAF. It was officially handed over to 8 Skuadron during a ceremony on 22 March 2017, the second day of the LIMA 2017 airshow on Langkawi Island, Malaysia. The four A400Ms, with c/n 022, 032, 036 and 050, received s/n M54-01 to M54-04. They were delivered on 12 March 2015, 27 December 2015, 11 June 2016 and 12 March 2017 respectively.

The maximum take-off weight of the C-130H is 155,000lbs (70,307kg) and its maximum allowable payload is 42,000lb (19,090kg). In comparison, an A400M has a maximum take-off weight of 310,852lb (141,000kg) and is capable of carrying a maximum 81,600lb (37,000kg) payload, which is almost twice that of the C-130H.

Despite having almost twice the payload capacity of C-130H, the A400M has a minimum tactical landing run of 770m (2,530ft) and minimum tactical take-off run of 980m (3,215ft), which is close to the C-130H/H-30's 750m minimum tactical landing run and 950m minimum take-off run. In addition, the A400M has twice the range of the C-130H and can receive fuel via its inflight refuelling (IFR) probe, whereas the C-130H/H-30s of the RMAF are not equipped with IFR probes.

Malaysia's A400M Fleet in Disaster Relief Operations

As of April 2023, the RMAF's A400Ms had logged eight years of operation. Since its introduction, the A400M has given a boost to strategic airlift as the core capability required to carry out air mobility tasks inside Malaysia, bridging Sabah and Sarawak with Peninsular Malaysia and across the globe. While the RMAF now possesses four A400Ms there is an obvious gap in strategic airlift requirements and capacity to be fulfilled in the coming years, making it possible for Malaysia to procure more A400Ms as a replacement for the current fleet of C-130H/H-30s.

The RMAF's A400Ms have been actively involved during Operation *Penawar* by sending the most needed supplies during the movement control order (MCO) periods and performing humanitarian assistance and disaster relief (HADR) missions, sending supplies especially to East Malaysia. Throughout the operation, the RMAF provided substantial support to many government agencies, including continuous logistic support to the Electoral Committee during the Sabah election in the midst of the COVID-19 pandemic in 2020, involving C-130H-30s from 14 and 20 Skuadrons.

Performing HADR has since become integral to the RMAF in support of the Malaysian government's stance in the Association of Southeast Asian Nations (ASEAN) region. The A400Ms travelled to Chittagong, Bangladesh and Cagayan de Oro, in the Philippines, sending relief and basic supplies to the affected people.

The A400M was used to send heavy equipment into tsunami-stricken Palu in Indonesia to reinforce the clean-up and rebuilding process. This has given HADR tasking a new meaning. Sorties generated to assist the rebuilding of Palu were not directly into the city. It was planned, from the onset, to reach Palu via Halim Perdanakusuma Air Base (Indonesian Air Force) as a staging point. A 22-tonne indigenously-built PT Pindad Excava 200 excavator and two Hino 300 trucks with 5000l capacity tanks was part of the load.

Keeping the A400M Fleet Airworthy

The operational tempo of the A400M has taken its toll, and each year the Skuadron has fulfilled the retrofit programme to ensure the continuity of strategic airlift and the new endeavour of tactical airlift capability.

After five years of operations, the A400M required a scheduled heavy maintenance and retrofit programme to meet the final standard operating clearance. The challenge at the Skuadron was to maintain aircraft availability as well as spares from the original equipment manufacturer. This situation will be manageable if RMAF obtains more A400Ms to maintain its capability on long-range strategic platforms.

The RMAF's Atlas fleet has enjoyed the greatest number of flying hours in the A400M worldwide fleet. This has been due to heavy dependency of the A400M on carrying out strategic airlifts domestically and internationally. In doing so, the engine operating hours and the aircraft flight cycle have become very critical, as the same aircraft is being used for multiple missions each day. This tempo has become the norm at every Langkawi International Maritime and Aerospace (LIMA) exhibition and Merdeka annual celebration. The engineering department has devised numerous mitigation measures in order to keep the aircraft flying.

Spares management for the A400M has always required dynamic forecasting and flexibility. No.22 Skuadron has had proper forecasting and trend monitoring in place. Based on the A400M minimum operational and safety equipment list, any required spares that were not covered under in-service support would be put on demand by the squadron. However, due to the high cost and arduous spares procurement requirements, the squadron devised a proactive forecast for each A400M, based on its engine operating hours, flight cycle, and aircraft's flight hours.

Future of the A400M Fleet

On 4 February 2022, the RMAF's No.22 Skuadron began a two-month-long restructuring programme. On 8 April 2022, a historic event was held in Subang and No.22 Skuadron was reformed as No.8 Skuadron. During the ceremony, Subang Air Base Commander, Brigadier General Omar bin Hj Dawami, delivered the No.8 Skuadron badge to Lieutenant Colonel Yusrizal bin Zain, Commanding Officer of the A400M Squadron.

As of April 2022, the RMAF's A400M fleet was still receiving Standard Operative Clearance (SOC) upgrades through the retrofit programme. By doing so, the maximum number of A400M aircraft at the squadron has been upgraded. Under RMAF's Capability Development 2055 (CAP 55) proposed in 2018, reform of the air force's transport capability is planned. A number of C-130H/H-30s will be upgraded while at least two more A400Ms will be purchased.

If the RMAF is given the option to add two additional A400M aircraft to the fleet, the tactical and logistical roles of the aircraft in No.8 Skuadron will be separated. The next aircraft would be fully utilised as dedicated mutil-role tanker transports (MRTT) by keeping their Cobham 908E Wing Dispense Equipment (WDE) pods, while the rest will be slated for a logistical role without a sophisticated Electronic Warfare (EW) suite to reduce the possibility of having the retrofit done overseas.

A three-ship arrowhead formation flight of three A400Ms with s/n M54-01, M54-02 and M54-03 during the opening ceremony of the LIMA 17 airshow, 21 March 2017. (Babak Taghvaee)

All four A400Ms of the RMAF participated in the LIMA 17 airshow in March 2017. M54-03 was one of them and flew during the opening ceremony on 21 March 2017. (Babak Taghvaee)

A400M with s/n M54-03 at Langkawi Island on 24 March 2017. (Babak Taghvaee)

TENTERA UDARA DIRAJA MALAYSIA
03

A400M with s/n M54-03 banking over Langkawi airport during a display flight on 21 March 2017. (Babak Taghvaee)

An A400M with s/n M54-02 is flying over Langkawi airport during a display flight on 21 March 2017. (Babak Taghvaee)

M54-04 is the fourth A400M of the RMAF, and was officially handed over to its squadron during LIMA 17 airshow in March 2017. (Babak Taghvaee)

During the LIMA 17 airshow in March 2017, this A400M with s/n M54-04 was handed over to No.22 Skuadron. (Babak Taghvaee)

The first A400M from the RMAF, with M54-01, was officially handed over to No.22 Skuadron during the LIMA 15 airshow in March 2015. (Babak Taghvaee)

Casa/IPTN CN-235-220M Fleet: 1999–Today

Today, seven Casa/IPTN CN-235-220M aircraft are in use by two squadrons of the RMAF in Kuching and Subang air bases. The aircraft were purchased from Indonesia between 1995 and 2002 and delivered between 1999 and 2006, and have been used for a variety of missions including tactical transport, VIP (Very Important Person) transport and Maritime Patrol. Among the seven CN-235-220Ms in service today, five are in use with No.1 Skuadron 'Courage' from for maritime patrol and transport tasks, while two are in use for cargo and troop transport at No.21 Skuadron 'Telan' (Swallow).

For decades, De Havilland Canada DHC-4A Caribou light transport aircraft played an important role transporting Malaysian Armed Forces' personnel and their equipment, weapons and ammunition across the country. After delivery of the C-130H/H-30s, the RMAF continued operating them until September 2020 when they were replaced by CN-235s. In the years between 1966 and 1973, the RMAF received 18 brand new DHC-4As from its Canadian manufacturer, which took the place of six Handley Page HPR-7 Herald 401 transport aircraft as well as several Scottish Aviation Twin Pioneer STOL utility aircraft.

The new examples received s/n FM1100 to FM1117 and were delivered to No.8 Skuadron in Labuan and No.1 Skuadron in Sungai Besi. Both of these squadrons had operated Twin Pioneer light transport aircraft and DHC-4s were their replacement. One, with s/n FM1101 (c/n 2546), crashed at Meligan airstrip in Sabah on 1 December 1967. Serial numbers of the remaining DHC-4As were changed to FM1401 to FM1416 in 1969. FM1409 (c/n 278) ditched into the sea at Cowie Bay, Sabah, on 30 March 1970.

DHC-4As of the RMAF played an important role in supporting operations of the Malaysian armed forces against Soviet-backed communist militias including the Malaysian National Liberation Army, which was supported by North Vietnam and then Vietnam between 1968 and 1989. DHC-4As airlifted Malaysian Army Rangers, their weapons, ammunition and equipment to most remote areas of the country. Thanks to their STOL characteristics, they could operate from short unpaved runways. The RMAF had one of them equipped with an M197 20mm Gatling gun to use as a gunship. Their use against communist militias resulted in a mortar attack of the Parti Komunis Malaya (PKM) or Malaysian Communist Party on its home base, Sungai Besi, on 31 March 1974, resulting in the destruction of one with s/n FM1413 (c/n 304).

In 1979, one more DHC-4A with s/n FM1405 (c/n 273) crashed into the sea; its wreckage was found by the US Navy's USS *Tarawa* amphibious assault ship and delivered to RMAF. Serial numbers of the remaining Caribous were changed to M21-01 and M21-18. M21-12 (c/n 280) was lost in an incident at Simanggang on 29 November 1980, followed by M21-17 (c/n 306) on 24 September 1982. The aircraft crashed about 23km (14 miles) from Brinchang in the Cameron Highlands while on a supply mission to Orang Asli settlement, Perak (Orang Asli village). All of its seven crew members were killed in the accident.

On 31 July 1995, M21-13 (c/n 281) crashed into the water near Labuan AB. It was recovered but was declared damaged beyond repair. Four years later, on 24 May 1999, the last DHC-4A accident happened to M21-05 (c/n 270) after it crashed into a swampy area at the end of the runway at Kuching Air Base following failure of one of the aircraft's engines during a regular training mission, killing all five crew members onboard. Finally, No.1 Skuadron in Kuching, which had been the last unit operating DHC-4As in the RMAF, had its last 11 Caribous retired in September 2000. At that time, only three were airworthy while eight others were stored awaiting buyers.

Back in 1993, when the RMAF still had 13 DHC-4As in service, decisions were made to order 32 Indonesian-built Casa/IPTN CN-235s as future replacements for the CN-235 fleet. This number was later reduced to 18 and in mid-1994 to only six. The first three CN-235 aircraft had originally been produced under licence by the Indonesian aircraft manufacturer Perseroan Terbatas Dirgantara Indonesia (PTDI) and entered operational service with the RMAF in August 1999 as medium-heavy tactical transport aircraft. With the delivery of three more CN-235s in late 1999 and early 2000, the remaining DHC-4As were retired. They received s/n M44-01 to M44-06. Two more CN235-220Ms, with s/n M44-07 and M44-08, were ordered in 2000 and were delivered in 2002 with VIP cabin configuration to be used by No.2 Skuadron at Subang, while the first six were divided between No.1 and 21 Skuadrons in Kuching and Subang respectively.

New Maritime Patrol Duty for the RMAF's CN-235-220Ms

On 9 August 2005, the RMAF received M44-07, the first VIP transport version CN-235-220M, following an order placed in November 2002. The second aircraft was delivered on 14 February 2006 and entered service with No.2 Skuadron 'Parakeet'. M44-07 was lost following a crash landing in shallow waters in a swampy beach area off Kuala Selangor, Malaysia on 26 February 2016. The aircraft caught fire and all of its eight crew members survived: a local fisherman who tried to help them drowned and lost his life.

The sole remaining VIP CN-235-220M with s/n M44-08 was later relieved of VIP transport duty and was formally transferred from No.2 Skuadron to No.1 Skuadron 'Courage' to be used for tactical transport duties in Kuching. The transfer took place on 17 May 2022 as a part of the RMAF's CAP 55 plan (Capability Development Plan 2055), which was presented in August 2018. Under the plan, RMAF's No.1 Skuadron could operate two aircraft for tactical transport and three for maritime patrol in two segments of the squadron by 2025.

In 2020, the US Naval Air System Command's (NAVAIR's) Security Cooperation Office and Naval Air Warfare Centre Aircraft Division's (NAWCAD's) AIRWorks department was awarded a contract through the US Navy to integrate Intelligence Surveillance and Reconnaissance (ISR) equipment into three CN-235-220Ms of the RMAF. The programme was facilitated by the US Navy's Building Partner Capacity programme in alignment with the US government's Maritime Security Initiative, enabling Malaysia to increase its security and awareness in the maritime domain within the Malaysian Exclusive Economic Zone (EEZ).

Under the programme, each CN-235-220MSA has been fitted with a maritime surveillance mission suite; maritime surveillance radar; line-of-sight datalink; an electro-optical/infrared (EO/IR) turret and a roll-on/roll-off mission system operator station. To further increase the RMAF's maritime intelligence, surveillance and reconnaissance (ISR) capabilities, compatible mobile and fixed ground control stations were also delivered.

On 3 August 2022, the US Navy announced the delivery of the first Airbus CN-235-220MSA to the RMAF after conversion in Indonesia. The aircraft, s/n M44-03 (c/n 036N) entered service with No.1 Skuadron in Kuching. M44-03 had logged its maiden flight after conversion in October 2021 but it took several more months until tests of its new systems were completed. On 7 October 2022, the second aircraft, with s/n M44-05 (c/n 038N), was delivered to the RMAF and entered service with No. 1 Skuadron. This was followed by delivery of the third CN-235-220MSA in 2023.

CN-235-220MSAs have taken the place of the three Beechcraft 200T King Air maritime patrol aircraft of No.16 Skuadron 'Canary' based in Subang. With the removal of C-130H-MPAs from maritime patrol duty in 1997, these Beechcraft 200Ts were primarily used for this purpose; however, due to their limited capabilities, they failed to meet the needs of Malaysia in monitoring the Malaysian exclusive economic zone (EEZ) particularly within the Malacca Strait.

The CN-235-220MSA are now the primary maritime patrol aircraft (MPA) of the RMAF. However, delivery of two Leonardo ATR-72MPAs, ordered in 2022, will mean the CN-235-220MSAs will no longer be the sole dedicated MPA of Malaysia. They are expected to become operational by 2026 and will be used primarily for maritime patrol duties over the Malacca Strait out of Subang. They will also carry out fishery protection and monitoring duties currently carried out by the three remaining Beech 200Ts. In addition to the two ATR-72MPAs, negotiations have been made for the possible procurement of four more ATR-72MPAs; however, as of April 2023, no order had yet been placed.

Above: M44-06, a CN-235-220M from No.21 Skuadron departing Langkawi International Airport on 22 March 2017. (Babak Taghvaee)

Right: M44-04, a CN-235-220M from No.21 Skuadron is flying over Kuala Lumpur during Malaysian Army Day parade on 21 September 2013. (Babak Taghvaee)

M44-01, a CN-235-220M from No.1 Skuadron at Langkawi International Airport in March 2017. (Babak Taghvaee)

M44-08, a CN-235-220M from No.1 Skuadron at Subang in August 2014 when it was still in use by No.2 VIP Skuadron. (Babak Taghvaee)

M21-04 (c/n 270) is a DHC-4A latterly on display at the RMAF Museum. (Babak Taghvaee)

Beech 200T King Air: 1994–2021

In October 1992, Malaysia ordered four Beech 200T King Air aircraft equipped with maritime surveillance radar to be used as replacements for the three C-130H-MPs in use with No.4 Skuadron. Equipped with Telephonics 143 search radar in the belly, as well as forward-looking infrared (FLIR), the Beech 200Ts enabled the RMAF to perform maritime patrol missions in the Malacca Strait and other areas of the Malaysian EEZ during the night and in all-weather conditions, while the C-130H-MPs could operate during the day as they lacked any FLIR system and maritime surveillance radar.

The RMAF continued operating its three C-130H-MPs primarily for maritime patrol duties until November 1997, when No.4 Skuadron was closed and two of its aircraft were chosen for conversion into KC-130H (C-130T), while its last remaining C-130H-MP was absorbed by No.20 Skuadron at Subang Air Base and has remained a reserve air asset of the RMAF for maritime patrol duties in the absence of the primary maritime patrol assets, the Beech 200Ts in the past and CN-234-220MSAs today.

The four Beech 200Ts with c/n BT-35/BB-1448, BT-36/BB-1451, BT-37/BB-1454 and BT-38/BB-1457 were sold by Beech Aircraft Corp to Hawker Pacific Pty Ltd of Yagoona, New South Wales, Australia, on 31 December 1993. After being fitted with a FLIR turret, surveillance radar and other equipment, the aircraft were flown to Subang AB in Malaysia via Paris-Le Bourget on 20 May 1994. They received s/n M41-01 to M41-04 and entered service with No.16 Skuadron 'Canary'.

Beech 200Ts could not meet the RMAF's needs for long-range and endurance maritime duties and as a result of that, Malaysia remained in need of a larger MPA for years until 2020 when the decision was made to convert three CN-235-220M tactical transport aircraft into MPAs. Two years later, two ATR-72MPAs were ordered with an option for possible procurement of four more examples.

In 2012, AIROD Aircraft Maintenance Repair and Overhaul Company was contracted to upgrade the four Beech 200Ts. As a part of the contract, all four aircraft had many of their components replaced with more modern equipment, including the installation of Telephonics RDR 1700B radar as a replacement for the old Telephonics 143 search radar. In addition, two of the Beech 200Ts were equipped with the Thales AMASCOS (Airborne Maritime Situation & Control System), a fully integrated airborne mission system for ground and maritime surveillance. The system became a useful asset of the aircraft for fishery control and anti-piracy missions in Malacca.

Following the disappearance on 8 March 2014 of Malaysia Airlines Flight 370 (MH370), a Boeing 777-2H6ER wide-body passenger aircraft with 9M-MRO registration code, carrying 227 passengers and 12 crew from Kuala Lumpur International Airport to Beijing Capital International Airport, No.16 Skuadron was the first RMAF unit tasked to take part in the search and rescue operation.

On 21 December 2016, the RMAF lost one of its four Beech 200Ts near Butterworth Air Base. The aircraft, with s/n M41-03, was about to land at the air base after a training mission but crashed on final approach, which killed one of the four pilots onboard. The remaining three aircraft in service with No.16 Skuadron were mainly used for fishery control missions in the Malacca Strait as well as other parts of the Malaysian EEZ in the last years of their service. The CN-235-220MSAs of No.1 Skuadron are now the RMAF's main MPA assets, having been in charge of that mission after Beechcraft 200Ts were retired in 2021. Soon, No.16 Skuadron will be reformed with two ATR-72MPA aircraft.

M41-02, a Beech (Beechcraft) B200T from No.16 Skuadron, landing at Subang on 16 September 2010. (Yuh Loh)

VIP Aircraft and Helicopter Assets of the RMAF

Throughout history, various helicopters and aircraft of the RMAF have been used to transport the Malaysian Royal Family as well as government officials. The aircraft and helicopters equipped with VIP cabin configuration have been historically operated by No.2 Skuadron 'Parakeet' at Subang, Kuala Lumpur. This squadron currently operates three aircraft and two helicopters.

Its aircraft include a civilian Airbus A319-112XCJ regional jet with 9M-NAA civil registration code, a Falcon 900 business jet with s/n M37-01 and a Bombardier Global Express 700 with s/n M48-02, while the helicopters comprise a pair of Sikorsky S-70A Black Hawks with s/n M46-01 and M46-02. In addition, a Fokker F28-1000 regional jet with s/n M28-01 and two S-61N-4 Nuri helicopters with s/n M39-01 and M39-02 are currently in possession of No.2 Skuadron and stored in its hangar.

The first aircraft of the RMAF, a former Royal Air Force Scottish Aviation Twin Pioneer 1 with c/n 529, was purchased for RM420,000 MYR in 1958 and was once used by Malaysian government officials for some of their flights. The aircraft arrived in Malaysia on 17 April 1958 and was welcomed by Tun Abdul Razak as Minister of Defence at Sungai Besi RAF station. Tunku Abdul Rahman, as Prime Minister, officially named the aircraft *Raja Wali*, after a famous eagle. It received s/n FM1001 five months later.

The aircraft was operated by No.1 Skuadron at Sungai Besi after official formation of the RMAF on 2 June 1958. *Raja Wali,* alongside other early pioneers of the squadron were used for liaison, transportation of troops to the front lines, transportation of patients, MEDEVAC (Medical Evacuation), CASEVAC (Casualty Evacuation), airdrop of PSYOPS (Psychological Operations) leaflets for communist militias in jungles. Thanks to their STOL (short take-off and landing) capability, these piston-engined aircraft could land on short unpaved runways in remote areas of Sabah and other parts of Malaysia.

The first jet aircraft of the RMAF dedicated to VIP transport missions were two Hawker Siddeley HS.125-400B business jets with c/n 25189 and 25209, each equipped with a pair of Rolls-Royce Viper 522 turbojets. They were capable of carrying six passengers in addition to two pilots. They received s/n FM-1200 and FM-1201 and were handed over to RMAF's No.4 Skuadron. Their serials were changed to FM-1801 and FM-1802 in January 1975 and then to M24-01 and M24-02 in the early 1980s. They were last operated by No.2 Skuadron before being retired in 1994.

HS.125s were too small for the long-distance flights of the Malaysia's Royal Family and as a result of that, Malaysia purchased two Fokker F28-1000 regional jets, which entered service with No.2 Skuadron as FM-2101 and FM-2102 on 5 February 1975. They were equipped with a pair of Rolls-Royce Spey Mk 555-15 turbofan engines and could carry around 50 passengers each. Their serial numbers were later changed to M28-01 and M28-02 in March 1984. M28-02 was withdrawn from service and sold, entering service with Air Niugini on 8 November 1988, while M28-01 remained in service until 2003 when a Boeing 737-7H6 with s/n M53-01 took its place. M28-01 is stored in No.2 Skuadron's aircraft hangar in Subang.

In June 1984, the RMAF's No.2 Skuadron received a brand new Canadair Challenger 600S business jet with c/n 1062. The aircraft, equipped with a pair of Lycoming ALF 502 turbofan engines received s/n M31-01 and remained in service until August 1989 when it was sold. It could carry 11 passengers in its cabin. As a replacement for that, the RMAF began using a Dassault Falcon 900 with s/n M37-01 (c/n 64). The aircraft, equipped with a pair of Garrett TFE731 turbofan engines, can carry 18 passengers, and is still in use by No.2 Skuadron today.

In 1997, No.2 Skuadron received a Bombardier CRJ200 regional jet with VIP cabin configuration. The aircraft, equipped with a pair of General Electric CF34-3A1 turbojet engines, remained in service for three years and was then sold back to Bombardier on 24 February 2000.

In 1999 and 2001, the RMAF began using two more Bombardier products. The first aircraft was a Bombardier Global Express business jet with c/n 9007 and equipped with two BR700-710A2-20 turbofan engines. It was delivered on 26 November 1999 and received s/n M48-01. The aircraft, capable of carrying 13 passengers, remained in service until 2002, when it was returned to Bombardier. In September 2002, No.2 Skuadron received a second Bombardier Global Express 5000 with c/n 9096, which received s/n M48-02 and is still in service with the squadron today.

In June 2003, No.2 Skuadron received a brand new Boeing 737-7H6 regional jet as a replacement for Fokker F28-1000 M28-01, which was retired after 28 years of service. The Boeing 737, with c/n 29274/397, received s/n M53-01. Equipped with two CFM56-7B27/B3 turbofan engines, it could carry almost twice as many passengers as the Fokker F28-1000 and remained in service until 16 May 2018, when it was sold to Kuwait International Company.

With the retirement of the Boeing 737 from service, the Malaysian government has used its Airbus A319-112XCJ with c/n 2949 for long-distance flights of its officials. The aircraft, with 9M-NAA registration code, is civilian-operated but its operations are coordinated by No.2 Skuadron. It has been used for this purpose since 14 December 2006. In addition, the RMAF's No.2 Skuadron also operated a Learjet 35A business jet with s/n M102-01 for government flights between 29 November 2013 and 5 October 2021.

Until 2022, the RMAF's No.2 Skuadron also operated CN-235-220M transport aircraft for VIP flights. Two were delivered in 2005 and 2006 and received s/n M44-07 and M44-08. M44-07 crash-landed into water due to technical failure on 26 February 2016, while M44-08 remained in service with the squadron until May 2022 when it was transferred to No.1 Skuadron to be used as a passenger aircraft. No.2 Skuadron retained a Bombardier Global Express, a Falcon 900 and a civilian-operated Airbus A319-112XCJ.

No.2 Skuadron has also operated two unusual aircraft in its history. They were a pair of Grumman G-111 Albatross (CSR-110 variant) amphibious aircraft equipped with VIP cabins. The two CSR-110s had been operated by the Royal Canadian Air Force from 1960 and 1970 and then by the Chilean Air Force between 1973 and 1980. They were directly purchased from Grumman Aerospace Corporation after their conversion to VIP specification took place. These two aircraft, with s/n M35-01 and M35-02, remained in service until 1993. M35-01 was latterly on display at the RMAF Museum, while M35-02 is preserved in RMAF's Ipoh Air Base.

No.2 Skuadron also operates a pair of Sikorsky S-70 Black Hawk helicopters and has two S-61N-1 VIP helicopters stored in its hangar in Subang. In the past, the squadron also operated an Aérospatiale/IPTN AS332L Super Puma with s/n M36-01, which crashed at Kampung Telok, Sungai Petani, Kedah, on 31 December 1993.

FM-1001, the first aircraft of the RMAF, was a Scottish Aviation Twin Pioneer named *Raja Wali*. It was latterly on display at the RMAF Museum. (Babak Taghvaee)

This DH.114 Heron 2D with s/n FM-1054 was used by the RMAF as a VIP aircraft during the 1960s. It is now at the closed Sungai Besi airfield, where the RMAF Museum was based until 2022. (Babak Taghvaee)

FM-1041 was one of two Cessna 310Fs purchased and received in 1961. It was named *Tirok*, while MF-1042 was named *Seindit* (Malaysia bird species). FM-1042 crashed during take-off from Sungai Besi, while FM-1041 was retired in 1964. They were both used for VIP flights of Malaysian government officials. FM-1041 was latterly on display at the RMAF Museum. (Babak Taghvaee)

M35-01 is one of two VIP cabin-equipped Grumman G-111 Albatross amphibious aircraft. It was latterly on display at the RMAF Museum. (Babak Taghvaee)

On the left is a Falcon 900 and on the right is the Global Express; the two S-70A Black Hawk helicopters in the middle are in use with No.2 Skuadron. (Royal Malaysian Air Force)

This Boeing 737-7H6 with s/n M53-01 was operated by No.2 Skuadron between 2003 and 2018. It is taking off from Subang on 20 September 2013. (Babak Taghvaee)

9M-NAA is a government-owned and civilian-operated Airbus A319-112XCJ with VIP cabin used by the Malaysian Royal Family. It is at Langkawi Island on 17 March 2015. (Babak Taghvaee)

M44-07 was one of two CN-235-220Ms from No.2 VVIP Skuadron, which received special marking on its tail for the occasion of its participation in Merdeka Day parade 2013. It is at Subang airport on 23 August 2013. It crashed into water on 26 February 2016. (Babak Taghvaee)

M44-08 was the second CN-235-220M from No.2 VVIP Skuadron; it is at Langkawi Island in March 2017. It was transferred to No.1 Skuadron in 2022. (Babak Taghvaee)

M46-01 is one of the two S-70A Black Hawk helicopters from No.2 VVIP Skuadron, based at Sungai Besi airfield until 2016. It is now the only airworthy helicopter in the squadron. (Geoff Russel)

M39-01 was one of two AS-61N-1 VIP helicopters used by No 2 Skuadron. It was last seen operational at Sungai Besi airfield, Kuala Lumpur, on 3 January 2011. It is believed to have been kept in service until 2018 when it was placed in storage. (Geoff Russel)

Chapter 3
Helicopter Fleet

Airbus Helicopters H225M (Eurocopter EC725AP) Super Cougar: 2012–Today

In the years between 1963 and 1969, the RMAF received SA-316B Alouette-III utility helicopters from its French manufacturer. They were widely used for missions ranging from search and rescue to attack, particularly during counter-insurgency missions. Surviving examples of these helicopters were later transferred to the newly formed Army Aviation Branch of the Malaysian Army and were used until they were replaced by Agusta A109K light utility helicopters.

The Super Puma, a descendant of the Super Cougar, became the second French-made helicopter to serve in the RMAF after the Alouette III. The history of the EC725AP Super Cougar with the RMAF starts in 1988 when an Aérospatiale/IPTN AS332L Super Puma with s/n M36-01 was delivered to fly government officials. Unfortunately, the VIP helicopter crashed into a swampy area near Kangar, Perlis, and four crew members lost their lives.

On 26 September 2008, the RMAF selected the EC725AP Super Cougar as a replacement for the RMAF's S-61A-4 Nuri helicopters. Together with the Italian Agusta Westland AW101, Russian Mil Mi-17 and American Sikorsky S-92, the EC725AP had taken part in the tender for the future replacement of the RMAF's large fleet of S-61A-4s. The initial plan was to procure 12 EC725APs as replacements for 12 existing S-61A-4s; however, the plan was abandoned after the country faced a financial crisis in October 2008. In April 2010, Malaysia finally purchased 12 Eurocopter EC725APs for the RMAF.

Powered by two Turbomeca Makila 1A4 turboshaft engines, the EC725AP Super Cougar is a long-range tactical transport helicopter designed for troop transport, casualty evacuation, combat search and rescue, maritime surveillance, humanitarian support, medical evacuation and shipborne operations. A derivative of the Eurocopter AS 532 Cougar, the EC725 features a five-blade composite main rotor incorporating a new airfoil shape to lower vibration levels, and is capable of carrying up to 29 passengers and two crew.

Subsequently, an order for 12 Eurocopter EC725AP Super Cougar helicopters (later known as Airbus Helicopters H225M) was placed for the RMAF. Following the RM1.6bn MYR order, the helicopters were delivered to the RMAF's No.10 Skuadron 'Elephant Tusk' at Kuantan and No.5 Skuadron 'Tiger' at Labuan between 2012 and 2014.

The helicopters, with s/n M55-01 to M55-12, were purchased to relieve the Sikorsky S-61A-4 Nuri utility helicopters from CSAR duty but, with the early retirement of the 50-year-old helicopters, they also undertook all of their predecessors' missions. Today, the RMAF uses its Super Cougar helicopters for CSAR but also humanitarian relief, MEDEVAC, SAR and also operations for RMAF Special Forces, known as PAKSAU (Pasukan Khas TUDM).

In 2013, the RMAF still had 28 S-61A-4 Nurei multi-purpose helicopters in its service. Almost half were operational simultaneously. Some of these helicopters were withdrawn from use as their missions were taken over by the EC725APs, while others were kept in service and underwent modernisation at AIROD in Subang. It was planned to retire the modernised helicopters by 2028 and replace them with additional H225Ms. However, following an increase in incidents and accidents of the Nuri fleet in 2019, the last 12 airworthy examples were retired in early 2020 without being replaced.

Eurocopter unveiled the first EC725 Cougar helicopter for the RMAF at the Marignane, France, factory on 6 December 2011. At that time, seven more helicopters were in various stages of production at Marignane. The first two EC725APs, with s/n M55-01 and M55-02, were flown to Malaysia and unveiled during a ceremony at Kuala Lumpur on 3 December 2012. M55-01 and M55-02 flew to Kuantan and were officially handed over to No.10 Skuadron during a formal ceremony on 2 January 2013.

The RMAF had planned to form a second squadron after the delivery of more EC725APs in 2013. Initially, it was planned to have No.7 Skuadron 'Rhino' at Kuching equipped with the Cougars as replacement for its ageing Nuris, but plans changed and No.5 Skuadron 'Tiger' at Labuan was selected to receive six EC725APs as a replacement for its last Nuri helicopters. Before delivery of these six to No.5 Skuadron in 2014, they were used for conversion training of the Nuri pilots of No.10 Skuadron.

Super Cougars In Action During Disaster Relief Operations

In the years between 1968 and 1979, the RMAF received 40 S-61A-4 Nuri utility helicopters from Sikorsky following four orders placed in 1968 (for ten), 1971 (for six), 1976 (for eight) and 1977 (for 16). These helicopters suffered 22 incidents and accidents resulting in the death of 71 people and the withdrawal of 19 of them from service. M23-16 was the last Nuri helicopter lost due to damages sustained during an emergency landing near Gubir Camp, Kedah, on 2 August 2019. At this point there were 12 airworthy Nuris still in service with No.3 Skuadron 'Hero' at Butterworth and No.7 'Rhino' Skuadron at Kuching. Some had been heavily upgraded between 2017 and 2019; however, safety concerns led to their early retirement.

Super Cougars were then called upon to carry out the missions previously carried out by the Nuris at Butterworth and Kuching. Subsequently, both squadrons each had one or two Super Cougars deployed to each one of these bases to undertake missions previously carried out by the Nuris. They were used for SAR, MEDEVAC and disaster relief operations, as well as medical and food resupply missions for people in villages with no access roads.

On 3 November 2020, an EC725AP of No.10 Skuadron participated in a joint SAR operation with three vessels and a CL-415 amphibious aircraft from the Malaysian Maritime Enforcement Agency (MMEA) to find and rescue a downed RMAF serviceman who had fallen into the waters of Endau near Sembilang Island. In December of that year, No.10 Skuadron participated in a disaster relief operation named *Murni*. Three different EC725APs from the squadron airlifted food supplies and basic living provisions for victims of a flood in the Kuala Lipis district. The majority of sorties were carried out by M55-06.

In February 2021, another EC725AP, this time belonging to No.5 Skuadron, was used to deliver food supplies and basic provisions to two longhouse settlements in Bintulu district, Sarawak, after they had been cut off from food supplies due to government-imposed movement restrictions during the COVID-19 pandemic. On 20 December 2021, a similar mission was carried out during another Operation *Murni* when M55-02 belonging to No.10 Skuadron airlifted 2.7 tonnes of food supplies for residents of the flood-affected Sungai Lembing. The next day, another Super Cougar from the same squadron evacuated four patients from two of the flood-affected villages, which had been cut off by flood. Two days after that, No.10 Skuadron was dispatched to evacuate an infant patient from a flood-affected village.

On 10 January 2022, an EC725AP helicopter from No.10 Skuadron was assigned to a mission to transport 13,896kg of food supplies to three aboriginal settlement areas in the Gua Musang district of Kelantan. Five days later, another Super Cougar participated in a two-day resupply operation led by the Commanding Officer of the Squadron, Lt Col Muhammad Fazri bin Md Zin. The squadron carried out 13 flight sorties by delivering 41,600kg of fuel supplies to the Telekom Malaysia (TM) telecommunication tower at Mount Telapak Buruk.

The EC725AP helicopters accumulated 20,000 flight hours up until February 2022 across various operations such as training and humanitarian missions, SAR, flood-relief and life-saving operations including during the COVID-19 pandemic. On 23 February 2022, several EC725AP pilots from No.5 and 10 Skuadrons received awards from Airbus Helicopters for scoring the highest flying hours on the helicopter in Asia. Some had logged 2,000 hours.

To keep the personnel of both squadrons at the highest state of readiness, both squadrons participate in annual exercises comprising four SAREX (Search and Rescue Exercises) involving deck landing and winch operations, one LIVEX (Live Firing Exercise), one CSAREX (Combat Search and Rescue Exercise) and one heliborne operation involving RMAF's PAKSAU (Airborne Special Forces). On 2 July 2022, five EC725APs from No.5 and 10 Skuadrons, alongside two AW139s, participated in exercise *Helo Hero* to carry out heliborne air assault and helicopter insertion and extraction (HIE) with 120 members of the Malaysian Army's (TDM) 10th Parachute Brigade.

M55-01 and M55-02, two EC725APs from the RMAF, have had their FLIR turrets installed during a display flight at the opening ceremony of the LIMA 2017 airshow. (Babak Taghvaee)

M55-10, one of 12 EC725APs, is at Langkawi Island in March 2015. (Babak Taghvaee)

M55-01 is another one of the 12 EC725APs and is at Langkawi Island in March 2017. (Babak Taghvaee)

Two EC725APs carry Malaysian flags during Malaysian Army Day parade at Kuala Lumpur on 21 September 2013. (Babak Taghvaee)

M55-02, with searchlight and FLIR installed, carries a Malaysian flag during the Malaysian Army Day parade at Kuala Lumpur on 21 September 2013. (Babak Taghvaee)

M55-04, with searchlight and FLIR installed, during the Malaysian Army Day parade at Kuala Lumpur on 21 September 2013. (Babak Taghvaee)

An EC725AP, with s/n M55-02, is in the foreground and a Malaysian Army Aviation AgustaWestland A109LOH is in the background during the LIMA 15 airshow on 17 March 2015. (Babak Taghvaee)

An EC725AP and two S-61A-4s fly with an RMAAC A109LOH and an RMNA AS555SN during the Merdeka (Independence) Day parade at Kuala Lumpur on 31 August 2013. (Babak Taghvaee)

AgustaWestland AW139: 2022–Today

The last 12 airworthy Sikorsky S-61A-4 Nuri utility helicopters in service with No.3 Skuadron at Butterworth and No.7 Skuadron at Kuching were retired from service in January 2020. Some, including M23-37, had been modernised by AIROD Sdn Bhd just a few years before in order to remain in service for at least ten more years. As a part of the modernisation work under 'NUP4' (Nuri Programme 4), the helicopters had most of their analogue instrumentation replaced with multifunction digital displays, new autopilot, auto-hovering system, and a new U/VHF radio system, but the crash of S-61A-4 s/n M23-16 in 2019, due to technical failure, led to the early retirement of the fleet.

The RMAF selected the AgustaWestland AW139, now known as the Leonardo AW139, as an immediate replacement for the Nuri helicopters and subsequently decided to lease four from WestStar Aviation Services Sdn Bhd. The 15-seat, medium-sized twin-engined helicopter was smaller than the Nuri; however, its flight characteristics and performance were greater, and it was more affordable to maintain and operate.

On 22 January 2022, the RMAF officially received its first two AW139 medium-lift helicopters with s/n M104-01 and M104-02. The other two were taken into stock by the RMAF on 22 February 2022 (s/n M104-03) and 22 April 2022 (s/n M104-04). During a formal ceremony at Butterworth AB, the first three AW139s were handed over No.3 Skuadron, a previous operator of S-61A-4 Nuri helicopters.

The lease is a four- to five-year long temporary solution until Malaysia buys 24 utility helicopters in two batches, with deliveries starting in 2026 or 2027. Initially, it had been planned to obtain 18 more

EC725APs (now H225M) with an approximate price of US$30m each, though the AW139 is a lighter and smaller utility helicopter with an approximate price of US$11m per airframe.

Since their introduction, the RMAF's AW139s have been involved in at-least four annual exercises including several with the EC725APs from No.5 and 10 Skuadrons. During the Field Training Exercise *Wira Helo 6/22* (Hero Helo 6/22), held between 27 June and 2 July 2022, two AW139s joined five EC725APs to carry out a variety of missions. Each training involved members of 10th Parachute Brigade of the Malaysian Army.

On 28 February 2023, an AW139, s/n M104-03, and an EC725AP, s/n M55-08, participated in the first RMAF's Air Mobility Tactical Operation (AMTOP) exercise. It was an integrated exercise combining elements of the Malaysian Army (TDM) and the Royal Malaysian Navy (RLDM). This exercise was planned and coordinated by the 1st Air Region Headquarters (MAWILUD 1) of the RMAF to be carried out in the training operation area around Kuantan, Gong Kedak, Mersing and Pangkor Island.

The exercise, from 19 to 28 February 2023, also tested and ensured that the air defence assets belonging to the RMDF, especially its transport aircraft and helicopters, namely the C130H, A400M, EC725AP and AW139, are capable of carrying out operational tasks on land and at sea. This training proved the ability and importance of interoperability of the Malaysian Armed Forces and their special forces elements including Special Operations Group (GGK), 10 Brigade Elite Team (Para), Marine Special Forces (PASKAL) and RMAF Special Forces (PASKAU).

M23-15 (c/n 61-781), a S-61A-4 from No 3 Skuadron, during the Malaysian Army Day parade, at Kuala Lumpur, on 21 September 2013. Later, the helicopter sustained severe damages during a crash-landing on a small island, and slid down a slope at Pulau Perak, Kedah, on 22 December 2013. (Babak Taghvaee)

Above: This S-61A-4, with s/n M23-22, belonged to No.3 Skuadron, and is seen during the Malaysian Army Day parade at Kuala Lumpur on 21 September 2013. The helicopter remained in service until January 2020. (Babak Taghvaee)

Left: M23-16 (c/n 61-783) was one of the last S-61A-4s of No.3 Skuadron. It is hovering over Merdeka Square, Kuala Lumpur, during the Malaysian Army Day parade, on 21 September 2013. The helicopter sustained severe damages during an auto-rotation landing due to engine failure, near Gubir Camp, Kedah, on 2 August 2019. This helicopter was one of several examples used in counter-piracy operations before 2013. (Babak Taghvaee)

M23-37 was a S-61A-4 from No.5 Skuadron that underwent modernisation at AIROD Sdn Bhd in 2016. It was handed over to the RMAF during a ceremony in Langkawi airport in March 2017. (Babak Taghvaee)

An upgraded S-61A-4 with s/n M23-37 attended LIMA 17 airshow in March 2017. It was equipped with four multi-function display panels as well as other modern avionic systems. (Babak Taghvaee)

The handover of the modernised S-61A-4 with s/n M23-37 by AIROD Sdn Bhd during the LIMA 17 airshow in March 2017. (Babak Taghvaee)

M104-01 to M104-04, all four AW139s leased by the RMAF, in front of the helicopter hangar of No.3 Skuadron at RMAF Butterworth on 21 March 2023. (Shay Rahman via Leonardo)

M104-03, one of four AW139s leased by the RMAF, in front of the helicopter hangar of No.3 Skuadron at RMAF Butterworth on 21 March 2023. (Shay Rahman via Leonardo)

M104-03 is one of four AW139s of the RMAF, inside the hangar of No.3 Skuadron at RMAF Butterworth on 21 March 2023. (Shay Rahman via Leonardo)

AW139 with s/n M104-04 landing at RMAF Butterworth in September 2022. (Jamil Jaafar)

M104-03, one of four AW139s leased by the RMAF in Butterworth AB, in March 2023. (Shay Rahman via Leonardo)

Chapter 4

Pilot Training

Piston-Engine Training Aircraft: 1958–2009

For decades, the RMAF has had domestic fixed-wing aircraft and helicopter pilot training capability. From 2018, the air force sent its future fighter pilots abroad to pass the Fighter-Lead in Training (FLIT) course, as it lacked enough operational advanced training jet aircraft to train them at home. The RMAF currently uses just 21 PC-7 Mk II Turbo Trainers for ab-initio and basic fixed-wing aircraft pilot training and just two Beechcraft 350i King Air twin-engine turboprop aircraft for transport aircraft pilot tactical training. There are five civilian-owned Airbus Helicopter EC120Bs for helicopter pilot training.

The first training aircraft used to train Malaysia's military pilots were ex-Royal Air Force de Havilland DH.82A Tiger Moth monoplanes in use by the Malaysian Auxiliary Air Force in Singapore. The aircraft were used for pilot training even before the official formation of the RMAF in 1958. One of them, with s/n T7275, crashed on 20 January 1957 due to engine failure at Serdang, Selangor, killing its civilian pilot Gilbert Manuel. In memory of T7275, Malaysia purchased another DH-82 with c/n 85592, which had been used by the RMAF as DE638 between 1942 and 1952. The DH-82 was rebuilt by British Aerospace plc at the request of the Malaysian government between February and October 1989. It arrived at Malaysia through Klang port on 23 November 1989 and was delivered to the RMAF Museum at Sungai Besi AB on 27 November. It was unveiled on 1 June 1990 with s/n T7245.

Upon the formation of the RMAF in 1958, the force used seven ex-RAF de Havilland Canada DHC-1 Chipmunks with s/n FM-1020 to FM-1026 as primary pilot trainers. A gradual changeover was made to Percival Provost T.51 training aircraft. FM-1020 crashed in 1959, while the remaining six Chipmunks were taken by Penang Flying Club to be used for training civilian pilots. One of them, with s/n FM-1022, was later returned to the RMAF to be displayed at Alor Setar Air Base's parade ground. It was then transferred to the museum in Sungai Besi.

In 1961 and 1962, the RMAF received 18 Provost T.51 training aircraft, which were the unarmed version of the Provost Mk 52. The T.51s were equipped with an Alvis Leonides 126 nine-cylinder air-cooled radial piston engine capable of producing 550hp (410kW) power. They were given s/n FM-1031 to FM-1049 and remained in service until they were replaced with 15 Bulldog Mk 102 primary flight trainers in 1971. The Bulldogs were given s/n FM-1220 to FM-1234, entering service with Pulatibang 1 (1 Flying Training Centre) at Alor Setar. FM-1220 and FM-1225 crashed in 1979 and 1981 respectively, and the rest were reserialled as M25-01 to M25-13 in 1984 and remained in service until 1992, when they were retired. Five were later privately owned by Aeroclub in Simpang.

In 1981, the RMAF purchased 44 PC-7 Turbo Trainer turboprop training aircraft from Pilatus Aircraft Co in Switzerland under a US$53m deal. The aircraft were delivered between 1982 and 1984 and were used by two training centres. Some were wired to carry and use weapons such as rocket and cannon pods for counter-insurgency and close-air-support missions and, because of that, they were painted in jungle camouflage. The aircraft were each equipped with a Pratt & Whitney Canada PT-6A-25A (750hp) turboprop engine and received s/n M33-01 to M33-44.

Fifteen of the PC-7s were withdrawn from use due to incidents and accidents between 1984 and 1993. The remaining 29 PC-7s were used for both ab-initio and basic pilot training after the retirement of the Bulldog Mk 102s. Before that, Bulldogs had been used for primary or ab-initio training of cadets in 1 FTC. To save money, the RMAF resumed using ultralight piston-engined aircraft for ab-initio training in 1995.

In 1993, MD-3-160 Swiss Trainer light training aircraft, equipped with the Lycoming O-320-D2A, 119 kW (160 hp) piston engine and designed by Dätwyler, a Swiss aviation company, were to be used as replacements for the Bulldog Mk 102s. SME Aerospace, a Malaysian company, acquired rights to build the aircraft from the Swiss company. Under licence, production of the aircraft named 'Aero Tiga' began, with deliveries to the RMAF taking place between 1995 and 1999. The RMAF received 20, serialled M42-01 to M42-20, which entered service with the 1 FTC in Alor Setar, effectively removing the PC-7s from the ab-initio or primary pilot training.

In addition, the RMAF received four Australian-designed and Malaysian-built Eagle 150B light training aircraft. Equipped with Teledyne Continental Motors IO-240-A four-cylinder air-cooled, horizontally-opposed piston engines capable of producing 93kW (125hp) power, the Eagle 150Bs had a similar use to the Aero Tigas in 1 FTC. These aircraft received s/n M51-01 to M51-04. One of them was converted into an unmanned aerial vehicle named Eagle ARV System, an optionally piloted aircraft developed by Eagle Aircraft Pty Ltd, BAE Systems and Composites Technology Research Malaysia (CTRM) for the Malaysian government. The remaining three Eagle 150Bs hadn't much service life and soon retired, with one of them finding its way into the RMAF Museum.

The use of the MD-3-160s for ab-initio was not a cost-saving solution for 1 FTC and subsequently, their number in service was reduced until they were all put into storage once the RMAF began using the PC-7s for this purpose from 2006. M42-01 and M42-12 are currently preserved at the RMAF Museum, 11 others are believed to be stored at the now closed Sungai Besi airfield, and seven others, which were officially retired in 2009, are stored in Alor Setar. After retirement of the MD-3-160s, the RMAF no longer used any piston-engined aircraft for primary or ab-initio fixed-wing aircraft pilot training. Today, 21 PC-7 Mk IIs, seven MB-339CMs and Beechcraft 350is are the only training aircraft of the force, although the MB-339CMs have been grounded since 2017.

This de Havilland DH-82 Tiger Moth training biplane with s/n T7275 was latterly on display at the RMAF Museum. (Babak Taghvaee)

This ex-Royal Thai Air Force DHC-1 Chipmunk represents FM-1022, one of six examples that served with the Malaysian Auxiliary Air Force and then the RMAF between 5 May 1957 and 1962. (Babak Taghvaee)

FM-1037 is one of the Percival Provost T.51s that served with the RMAF between 1961 and 1971. Latterly on display at the RMAF Museum, it can be seen in Sungai Besi airfield where the museum was located until 2022. (Babak Taghvaee)

M25-08 is one of two retired Bulldog Mk 102 training aircraft latterly on display at the museum. Here it is in the old museum location at Sungai Besi in August 2013. (Babak Taghvaee)

M42-12 is one of the MD-3-160s used by the RMAF between 1995 and 2009. It was latterly on display at the RMAF Museum. (Babak Taghvaee)

This Eagle 150B training aircraft, with s/n M51-01, was converted into a surveillance UAV by Eagle Aircraft Pty Ltd, BAE Systems and Composites Technology Research Malaysia (CTRM) for the Malaysian government during a research project. It was latterly on display at the air force museum. (Babak Taghvaee)

Pilatus PC-7 Mk II Turbo Trainers: 2001–Today

In the late 1990s, the RMAF suffered from a lack of PC-7s, as 16 of them were lost due to incidents and accidents between 1984 and 1999, leaving only 28 for the 1 FTC at Alor Setar. The 20 MD-3-160s, which the centre received between 1995 and 1999, as well as three Eagle 150Bs, were used for primary pilot training in order to reduce pressure on the PC-7 fleet until its increase in the following years.

As a replacement for the lost PC-7s, Malaysia considered buying the PC-7 Mk II. They were equipped with the more powerful PT6A-25C, which was capable of producing 522kW (700shp) power. The PC-7Mk II had been developed by Pilatus for the South African Air Force and was constructed using the PC-9 airframe with elevated aft seat for the instructor pilot, providing better visibility, particularly during take-off and landing. The PC-7 Mk II retained the wing and external stores (hard points) of the PC-7 so it was a cost-effective option for the air force.

Following a three-year delay, nine PC-7 Mk IIs were finally ordered under a US$28–35m contract in 2000, with deliveries taking place in 2001. They were serialled M50-01 to M50-09. One of them, s/n M50-04 (c/n 611), was lost in an accident on 2 January 2002. All of them were put into service with Pulatibang 3 (3 FTC) at Kuantan Air Base, while the PC-7s remained in use of Pulatibang 1 (1 FTC) in Alor Setar. PC-7 Mk IIs remained in use by 3 FTC until Alenia Aermacchi MB-339CM advanced jet trainers began taking their duty in 2009.

Under a 70m CHF (US$87.5m) order placed in 2006, Pilatus supplied the RMAF with ten more PC-7 Mk IIs in 2007, serialled as M50-10 to M50-19. Five more examples were ordered in 2014 with deliveries taking place in 2016. They received s/n M50-20 to M50-24. While all PC-7 Mk IIs had been painted in a white/red paint scheme, the last five were painted in red with blue and yellow stripes/flashes. They also had more advanced avionic systems with digital instrumentation instead of the analogue gauges mostly found on older examples. With the deliveries of M50-20 to M50-24, the last surviving PC-7 Mk Is of 1 FTC were retired from service.

According to satellite images, 25 PC-7 Mk Is were stored outside the aircraft sheds of 1 FTC and 2 FTC at Alor Setar. Out of these, 21 are still stored there while several have been put on display in various locations around Malaysia. On 16 September 2021, the Malaysian Ministry of Defence approved a request to display a PC-7 Mk I at the RMAF Academy in Padang Kawad. An aircraft was subsequently chosen and transferred, and was unveiled as a monument on 30 December 2021.

The RMAF has always had PC-7s participate in airshows, particularly LIMA at Langkawi Island. Five PC-7 Mk Is were formed into a display team named 'Tamin Sari', populated by instructor pilots from 1 FTC in 1983. The number was reduced to just three in 1993. In 1995, two of the team's aircraft accidentally collided in mid-air during an airshow, but their pilots successfully ejected and survived.

On 11 September 2009, a PC-7 Mk II with s/n M50-12 crashed at Langkawi airport during a rehearsal for an airshow, killing both pilots. On 25 March 2010, s/n M50-14 crashed during an airshow near University Utara Malaysia (UUM), Kedah, killing the pilot. On 11 January 2019, another PC-7 Mk II was withdrawn from service. The aircraft, with s/n M50-07, suffered damage to its main landing gear after an emergency landing next to the runway at Alor Setar Air Base, with the cause attributed to engine failure. The student pilot onboard saved the aircraft and it is currently under repair.

Some of the 21 PC-7 Mk IIs have been selected to be sent to Pilatus' factory to be re-airframed at the end of the fuselage's life. In 2022, Pilatus performed re-airframing on M50-01 and M50-02 and at the same time installed new avionic systems on the new airframe. Re-airframing of seven more PC-7 Mk IIs is currently taking place in Switzerland.

Taken on 23 July 2007, this photograph shows two PC-7 Mk IIs flying in Switzerland before delivery. (Pilatus Aircraft Corporation)

M50-22 and M50-23, two of the last batch of five PC-7 Mk IIs delivered to RMAF in 2016, during a photoshoot at Switzerland that year. (Pilatus Aircraft Corporation)

The formation flight of seven PC-7 Mk IIs during the opening ceremony of LIMA 17 on 21 March 2017. (Babak Taghvaee)

Above: From front to the end, M50-05, M50-01, M50-02 and M50-08, four of seven RMAF PC-7 Mk IIs that flew in a seven-ship arrowhead formation flight at the opening ceremony of the LIMA 17 airshow on 21 March 2017. (Babak Taghvaee)

Left: This PC-7 Mk II with s/n M50-02, at Langkawi Island on 21 March 2017, was sent to the Pilatus aircraft factory for re-airframing in 2022. (Babak Taghvaee)

The RMAF's PC-7 Mk II with s/n M50-02 after changing its fuselage and during an engine test at Pilatus's aircraft factory in December 2022. (Django Bruinink)

Aermacchi MB-339CM: 2009–18

In 1969, Australia donated ten ex-RAAF CAC-27/Sabre Mk-32 fighter jets to the RMAF and six more two years later. They became the first fighter jets in the air force and remained in service until they were replaced with Northrop F-5E Tiger IIs just a few years later. To train their pilots, RMAF used 20 Canadair CL-41G-5 Tebuan (Wasp) training jet aircraft. They received s/n FM-1120 to FM-1139. All of the aircraft could be armed with rocket pods and unguided bombs and were used for close air support by No.6 and 9 Skuadrons at Kuantan. Two of them were also used for photo-reconnaissance and surveillance before the delivery of two RF-5E Tiger Eyes to RMAF.

Nine CL-41G-5s were lost in incidents and accidents between 1969 and 1983. The surviving examples were re-serialled from M22-01 to M22-11 in 1983. M22-11 was later withdrawn from use due to a technical failure during a test flight 16km northeast of Kuantan on 5 March 1983. Both test pilots onboard ejected and survived. The remaining ten CL-41G-5s were retired from service in 1986. Out of these, M22-07 to M22-10 were later sold to civilian customers while the rest are preserved. M22-01 is in the RMAF Museum while the rest can be found in various museums and air bases across the country.

As a replacement for the CL-41G-5s, 12 Aermacchi MB-339AMs were ordered in 1982 with their deliveries taking place in 1983 and 1984. They received s/n M34-01 to M34-12. M34-06 was lost in an accident on 14 July 1985 and as a replacement, an additional example was ordered in 1985, which was delivered in the same year and given s/n M34-13. The aircraft were put into service with 15 Skuadron at Kuantan and were used by 3 FTC for both FLIT (Fighter Lead-In Training) and counter-insurgency, as they could be armed. After their deliveries, No.6 and 9 Skuadrons, which operated CL-41G-5s, saw their aircraft dedicated mostly to the combat missions until their retirement in 1986.

Four more MB-339AMs were lost in incidents and accidents before withdrawal of the type from RMAF service:

On 14 December 1995, No.15 Skuadron lost M34-09 (c/n 6707) after its pilot, 24-year old Lieutenant Effendy Jalani, ejected on the runway at Butterworth during his first solo flight after he lost control of the aircraft during take-off. The aircraft was damaged and was withdrawn from service.

On 15 April 1996, M34-08 (c/n 6700) suffered serious airframe failure during a rocket-training attack on a small rock in the South China Sea. The pilots ejected safely after the aircraft stalled and entered spin at 2,000ft altitude, 30nm off Mersing. Both pilots were rescued.

On 27 October 1998, M34-04 (c/n 6696) crashed in Piah Forest Reserve in Perak after its pilot, 28-year-old Lieutenant Khvril Falei Amdan, ejected safely after losing control during an air-combat manoeuvring mission against two Hawk Mk 108s.

On 23 January 2002, another MB-339AM with s/n M34-07 (c/n 6699) was lost. It crashed at the edge of Kenering water catchment after engine failure. The instructor and student ejected and landed in Kenering Lake, from where they were rescued. MB-339AM was powered by a Rolls-Royce Viper 632-43 turbojet engine capable of producing 17.8kN (4,000lbf) thrust.

No.15 Skuadron had only two of the seven airworthy MB-339AMs left by 2002, forcing Malaysia to plan for the acquisition of more examples for LIFT. In May 2003, Malaysia negotiated with New Zealand to obtain 17 MB-339CBs previously operated by the Royal New Zealand Air Force but this didn't bear any fruit. Later the Malaysian Ministry of Defence entered negotiations directly with the Italian aircraft manufacturer to buy eight brand new MB-339CDs to complement the existing seven MB-339AMs.

Later, an improved variant named MB-339CM, equipped with contemporary Avionic systems and IFR probe, was ordered from Alenia Aermacchi on 22 November 2006. The first aircraft of this order, which received s/n M34-14, logged its maiden flight on 25 January 2009. Together with the second aircraft, M34-15, it was flown to Kuantan AB, home of 3 FTC on 1 March 2009. Deliveries continued until 2 December 2009, when the last two, M34-21 and M34-21, arrived at Kuantan.

The RMAF had all of its MB-339AMs, which had been shared between No.15 Skuadron at Butterworth and 3 FTC at Kuantan, retired by December 2009. M34-12, which had been grounded for years, was delivered to the RMAF Museum, while M34-01 was preserved at Butterworth. M34-09 ended up at the University of Science of Malaysia to be used as an instrumental airframe in Nibong Tebel, while the rest, including M34-02, M34-03, M34-05 and M34-10, were put into storage in Kuantan and were cannibalised for their useful parts.

Unlike MB-339AMs, which were also shared with No.15 Skuadron in Butterworth, MB-339CMs were only used by 3 FTC in Kuantan. No.15 Skuadron used the Hawk Mk 108 for fighter-pilot training. On 17 May 2016, M34-20 crashed in a paddy field at Pahang near Nenasi. The instructor and student ejected and survived. The cause of the crash was engine failure, which later spread to the fleet and grounded all seven MB-339CMs in 2018.

With the MB-339CMs grounded without replacement, the RMAF began using the small fleet of Hawk Mk 108s from No.15 OCU Skuadron for LIFT until 21 November 2021 when one, serialled M40-08, crashed. This reduced the number of Hawk Mk 108s to just five, with three kept airworthy simultaneously, which together were only enough for routine conversion flight training of new Hawk Mk 208 pilots.

In 2020, the RMAF began sending some of its future fighter pilots to Canada to undergo FLIT training. In 2020, eight student pilots were sent to Canada to pass the FLIT course while in 2021, ten more were sent. These students passed their FLIT at International Test Pilots School (IPTS) in Ontario. IPTS is currently an operator of two Aero L-29 Delfin, four L-39C Albatros and a Hawker Hunter T75 training jet. With the delivery of 18 FA-50 light combat aircraft (LCA) and TF-50A fighter lead-in trainers (FLIT) which were ordered on 24 February 2023, the RMAF will once again resume its domestic FLIT.

This CL-41G-5 Tebuan with s/n M22-04 is currently one of the few surviving examples in Malaysia. It was latterly on display at the RMAF Museum. (Babak Taghvaee)

M34-12 is one of a few surviving MB-339AMs, latterly on display at the RMAF Museum. (Babak Taghvaee)

MB-339CM with s/n M34-20 is at Langkawi International Airport during the LIMA 13 airshow in March 2013. (Babak Taghvaee)

Beechcraft 350i King Air: 2013–Today

The RMAF trains its transport aircraft pilots domestically. For that purpose, two Beechcraft 350i King Air twin-engine turboprop aircraft with s/n M101-01 and M101-02 have been in use at the Tactical Transport Flight Training Centre (PLTT) at Subang. The two aircraft were leased from Aerotree Defence & Services Sdn Bhd in 2013 for RM41.6m MYR, for a period of five years. This leasing contract has been extended several times and the aircraft are still in use training future transport aircraft pilots.

In 2013, the two Beechcraft 350is took the place of the last two airworthy Cessna 402Bs for transport aircraft pilot training with 1 FTC. They were the only surviving examples of the 12 Cessna 402Bs purchased in 1974 and delivered a year later. These aircraft, with s/n M27-01 to M27-12, were put into service with No.2 and No.20 Skuadrons in the 1980s, for liaison, VIP and troop transport as well as aerial surveillance or cartography. Four were equipped with a special hatch allowing installation of aerial cartography cameras in the aircraft.

In 1975, Cessna 402Bs took the place of three de Havilland DH-104 Dove 8s, with s/n FM-1051 to FM-1053, in use at 1 FTC, and its three DH.114 2D (former Royal New Zealand Air Force Devon C.1s) with s/n FM-1601 to FM-1603, in use with No.2 and 20 Skuadrons.

Three of the Cessna 402Bs were later lost in incidents and accidents. On 3 February 1985 in bad weather, M27-01 (c/n 402B0893) crashed into Bukit Ibol Hill, 12km east of Lawas on the Sabah-Sarawak border. Eight passengers and crew were killed. On 13 October 1993, M27-03 crashed and exploded at the New Salak South Village shortly after take-off, killing two pilots, and M27-02 (c/n 402B0871) was damaged and later withdrawn from service after its left main landing gear collapsed in September 2009. M27-02 was later sent to the RMAF Museum and M27-04 joined it in 2013.

This DH.104 Dove 8 with s/n FM-1051 was used for transport and training duties until replaced with the Cessna 402Bs. This example was latterly on display at the RMAF Museum at the now closed Sungai Besi airport. (Babak Taghvaee)

M27-04 is one of two Cessna 402Bs at the RMAF Museum. (Babak Taghvaee)

M27-02 was damaged due to the collapse of its left main landing gear while taxiing at Subang in September 2009. This Cessna 402B was not repaired, instead being transferred to the RMAF Museum. (Babak Taghvaee)

This Beechcraft 350i King Air with s/n M101-01 is currently one of two examples in use for tactical transport aircraft pilot training. It is at Langkawi Island on 23 March 2017. (Babak Taghvaee)

This Beechcraft 350i King Air with s/n M101-02 is one of two examples in use for tactical transport aircraft pilot training. It is at Langkawi Island on 17 March 2015. (Babak Taghvaee)

Airbus Helicopters (Eurocopter) H120B (EC120B): 2015–Today

The RMAF currently uses five Airbus (Eurocopter) H120B (EC120B) Calibri light helicopters with s/n M103-01 to M103-05 for domestic helicopter pilot training with 2 FTC at Alor Setar. The first helicopters used for pilot training were nine Bell 47G-5As, which were purchased from the US in 1974 and were delivered in the same year. These helicopters received s/n FM-2000 to FM-2008. Among them, FM-2001 crashed before 1983 and the rest were re-serialled from M26-01 to M26-08. These helicopters were used for primary and basic training, while SA-316Bs were used for complementary training.

The RMAF has received 33 Alouette III helicopters from France and Singapore. The first 13 were SE 3160 Alouette IIIs ordered in 1963 and delivered later that year and in 1964. Eight more were ordered in 1965, with their deliveries taking place in 1966, while five more were ordered in 1968 and received in 1969.

In addition to the 26 SE-3160s purchased from France, the RMAF received seven secondhand SA-316Bs from the Singaporean Air Force, which had been retired from their search-and-rescue duty in 1977. RMAF relied on its Alouette III helicopters for MEDEVAC, CASEVAC, SAR, CSAR, assault and even attack roles. Some of these helicopters were equipped with heavy machine guns and were used in conjunction with S-61A-4 Nuri utility helicopters (as their gunship escort) during counter-insurgency operations in the 1960s and 1970s. Several of them were lost to light and heavy arms fire.

The RMAF's Alouette III helicopters were used by No.3, 7 and 10 Skuadrons at Butterworth, Kuching and Subang, respectively, while some were loaned to 2 FTC at Alor Setar. After the establishment of the

Malaysian Army Air Corps (RMAAC/TDDM) on 13 March 1997, most of the surviving Alouette IIIs of RMAF (ten examples) were transferred to its No.881 Skuadron at Keluang and were used to provide air support for the army's rapid response force, including air transport, reconnaissance and tactical support. The RMAF continued operating several Alouette IIIs for pilot-training purposes as well as training pilots of the RMAAC and Royal Malaysian Navy Aviation (RMNA) at 2 FTC.

With the retirement of the Bell 47G-5As, the RMAF used its MD3-160 light training aircraft for primary flight training of its future helicopter pilots at 1 FTC in the late 1990s and early 2000s. Once graduated, the helicopter student pilot trained on Alouette IIIs at 2 FTC. This training stopped after the retirement of the MD3-160s. Subsequently, the complete training programme was performed on the Alouette IIIs until they were withdrawn from service.

In 2014, 2 FTC had six airworthy Alouette IIIs with s/n M20-06, M20-17, M20-18, M20-25, M20-28 and M20-29. With the delivery of the first two H120Bs in January 2015, M20-06 and M20-28 were withdrawn from use in that year, while the remaining four examples were retired in March 2016. On 3 December 2015, the RMAF officially unveiled its first H120Bs during a ceremony at Subang airport.

After the end of conversion training of the former Alouette III instructor pilots on the H120Bs, these five H120B helicopters were supplied by Gading Kasturi Sdn Bhd under a RM120m MYR Private Finance Initiative (PFI) deal. The Gading has provided total engineering and logistics support to five Airbus H120B helicopters and one H120B simulator through the Company Own Military Operates (COMO) concept for its basic helicopter flying school. The programme also involved in-house upgrading of the EC120B to fully glass cockpit and Night Vision Imaging Systems (NVIS).

M26-08 is a Bell 47G-5As used for helicopter pilot training in the 1970s and 1980s. It currently belongs to the RMAF Museum. (Babak Taghvaee)

M20-05 is an SE-3160 Alouette III helicopter, used by the RMAF until 2016. This example belongs to the RMAF Museum and is pictured here in its previous location at Sungai Besi airfield in August 2013. (Babak Taghvaee)

M103-04 is one of five H120B Calibri training helicopters of the MAF's 3 FTC at Alor Setar. (Royal Malaysian Air Force)

Other books you might like:

Air Forces Series,
Vol. 8

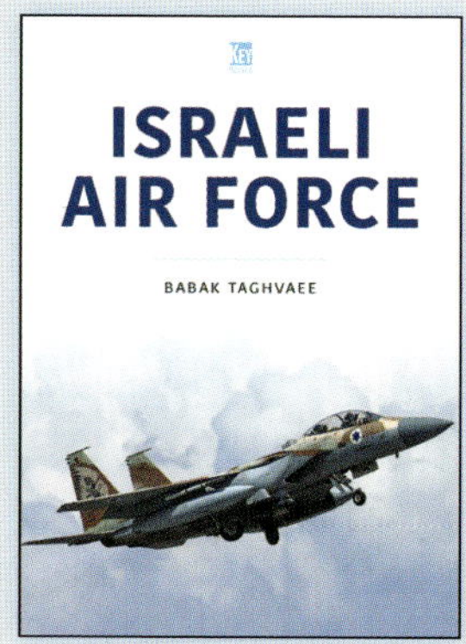

Air Forces Series,
Vol. 10

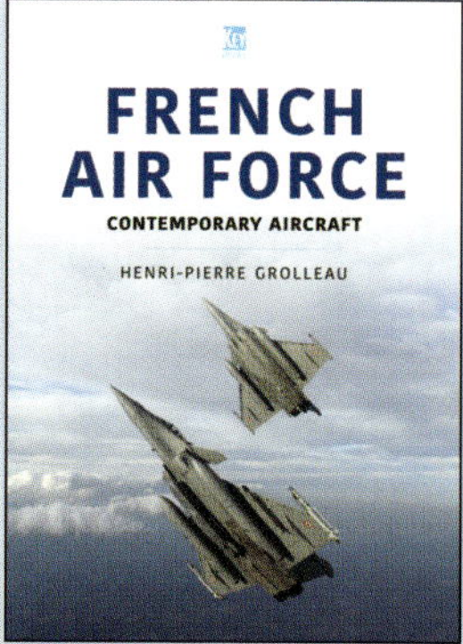

Air Forces Series,
Vol. 9

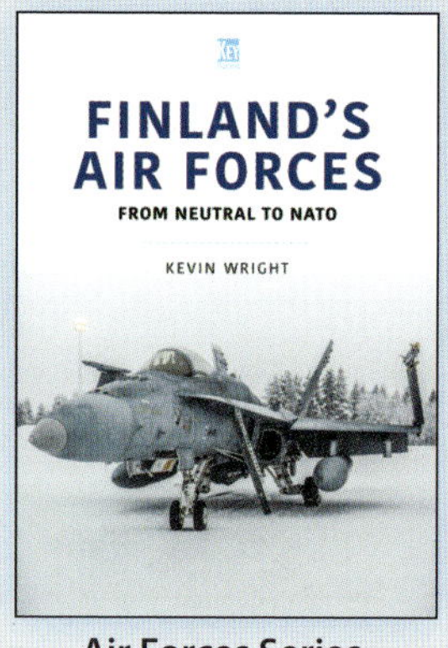

Air Forces Series,
Vol. 6

Air Forces Series,
Vol. 3

Airlines Series,
Vol. 13

For our full range of titles please visit:
shop.keypublishing.com/books

VIP Book Club

Sign up today and receive

TWO FREE E-BOOKS

Be the first to find out about our forthcoming
book releases and receive exclusive offers.

Register now at **keypublishing.com/vip-book-club**

Our VIP Book Club is a 100% spam-free zone, and we will never share your email with anyone else.
You can read our full privacy policy at: privacy.keypublishing.com